Sunshine Coast

A Place to Be

Sunshine Coast
A Place to Be

Rosella Leslie

Heritage
House

Copyright © 2001 Rosella Leslie

National Library of Canada Cataloguing in Publication Data

Leslie, Rosella M., 1948-
    The Sunshine Coast

    Includes index.
    ISBN 1-894384-19-9

    1. Sunshine Coast (B.C.) I. Title.

FC3845.S95L47 2001   971.1'31   C2001-910494-4
F1089.S94L47 2001First edition 2001

Heritage House acknowledges the financial support of the Government of Canada through the Book Publishing Industry Development Program (BPIDP) for our publishing activities. Heritage House also acknowledges the support of the British Columbia Arts Council.

Cover and book design by Darlene Nickull
Edited by Terri Elderton
Cover photos courtesy of <www.photographytips.com>
Front cover: Howe Sound looking northwest from Gower Point in Gibsons. Small photo is the beach at Davis Bay.
Back cover: Roberts Creek outlet (top left); sailboat lessons at the mouth of Wakefield Creek in West Sechelt, looking across Trail Bay towards Davis Bay in the background (top right); Davis Bay pier (middle left); Gibsons sailboats—from the Government wharf, looking towards Gambier Island (bottom left).

HERITAGE HOUSE PUBLISHING COMPANY LTD.
Unit #108 - 17665 66 A Ave., Surrey, B.C. V3S 2A7

Printed in Canada

The Canada Council | Le Conseil des Arts
for the Arts | du Canada

Dedication

This book is dedicated to my parents,
the late Thelma and Earle Leslie.

Acknowledgements

This book could not have been written without the help of people who either provided me with information or led me to another source. I would like to express my gratitude to all of those who helped me on this journey, including:

Graham Allen; Bob Anstead, Chapman Creek Fish Hatchery; Patsy Baker, Pender Harbour Garden Club; Tom Barker, Garden Bay Sailing Club; Ruth Beatty, St. John's United Church; Pat Beninger; Sam Bowman, Pearl Seaproducts Inc.; Gail Bull, Sunshine Coast Festival of the Written Arts; Pascal Carrara, Sunshine Kayaking; Mike Clements, Sunshine Coast Maritime History Museum; Lenore Conacher, Gibsons School of the Arts; Chuck Cookney, Construction Aggregates Ltd.; Alan Crane, Coast Recital Society; Doris Crowston, Sunshine Coast Arts Council; Marshall Davies; Bob Dixon, Davis Bay Sports Fishing; Trent Dixon, Sechelt Indian Band; George Drew; Pat Drope, St. Bartholomew's Anglican Church; James Eke, *Coast Reporter*; Scott Elliott, Trout Tales; Bob Ethridge; Doris Farrand, Sunshine Coast Power Squadron; Trevor Fawcett, Sunshine Coast Regional District (SCRD) Mapping Department; Paul Fenwick, Sunshine Coast Regional District; Brian Fawkes, Sunshine Coast Marine Rescue; David Foss, Harbour Authority of Pender Harbour; Carol Gardarsson, *Coast Independent*; Ann Gibb, Sechelt Lawn Bowling Club; Art Giroux, Tzoonie Outdoor Adventures; Alan Greene; Dorian Gregory, Sunshine Coast Amateur Radio Club; William "Billy" Griffith; Vicky Haberal, Ministry of Environment, Lands & Parks; Jo and Richard Hammond; David Harding; Deb Hodgkin, Sechelt Downtown Business Association; Tony Holmes, Artificial Reef Society; Lenora Inglis; Al Jenkins, Ministry of Environment, Lands & Parks; Hubert Joe; Miranda Joe, tems swiya museum; MaryEllen Johnson, Sechelt Garden Club; Pamela Kaatz, Howe Sound Pulp & Paper Ltd.; Bobby Kelly, Sechelt Garden Club; Tom Kershaw, Sunshine Coast Philharmonic Orchestra; Chris Kluftinger, Pender Chief Charters; Bob

Lemeux; Tracy "Tara" Lenec; Gordon Leslie; Gail Lewis, Elphinstone Pioneer Museum; Peter Light; Marta MacKown; Carol MacLeod, Sunshine Coast Equestrian Club; Kenan MacKenzie, Sunshine Coast Equestrian Club; June Malaka; Margaret McCaughan-Morrison; Laurie McConnell, Bad Dog Design; Susan Milne, Creekside Stables; Ken Moore, Coast Guard Auxiliary; Margaret Morris; Gail Mulcaster, Gibsons Lanes; Darlene Nooski, Sechelt Indian Band Salmon Hatchery; Laurie O'Byrne, Gumboot Garden Café; Katherine Patterson; Tamara Perry, Beldis Fish Co.; Brian Peterson, Scouts Canada; Tom Poulton, Sunshine Coast Hockey Association; Anne Quinn; Bea Rankin; Geoff Reed, Sunshine Coast Music Festival; Ken Robinson, Sunshine Coast Arena; Greg Russell, Roberts Creek Garden Club; Don Shin; Scott Shoemaker, Halfmoon Bay General Store; Des Sjoquist, School District No. 46; Eric Small; Peggy Small, Gibsons School of the Arts; Eve Smart; David Smethurst, Gibsons Yacht Club; Bob Stanhope, Sunshine Coast Inter-School Mountain Bike Race; Billie Steele; Angie Terrillon, Gibsons Garden Club; John Thomas, Coast Cable Communications Ltd.; Reg Thomas; Karin Tigges, Suncoast Raquet Club; Levi Timmerans, Department of Fisheries & Oceans - Small Harbours Branch; Kathryn Travers, Sunshine Coast United Mountain Bikers; Pearle Tretheway; Maria Van Dyk, Gambier Island Conservancy; Cynthia Von Rhau, Gibsons Beautification Committee; Juanita Wannamaker, Gibsons Curling Club; Ann Watson, Sechelt Community Archives; Myrtle Winchester, Harbour Spiel; and Lola Westell.

In addition, I thank the participants of the Elphinstone Pioneer Museum Oral History Project: Caryl Cameron, Isabel Gooldrup, Cledia Duncan, Eileen Griffith, Robert McKay, James Warnock, and Wilfred "Tiffy" Wray.

I am especially grateful to my fellow writers, Betty Keller, Maureen Foss, Gwendolyn Southin, Dorothy Fraser and Leslie MacFarlane, for their superb critiquing and constant encouragement.

Contents

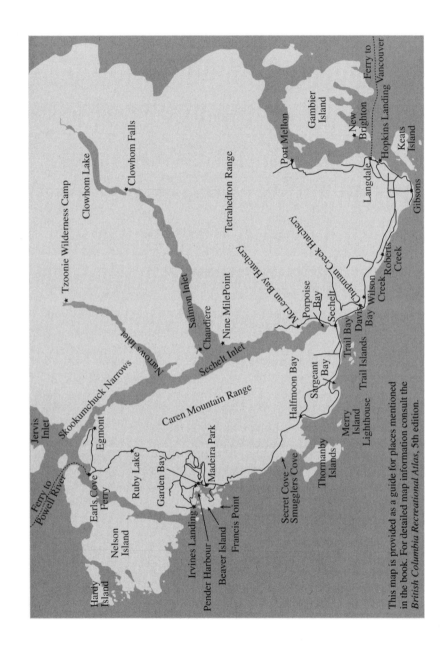

This map is provided as a guide for places mentioned in the book. For detailed map information consult the *British Columbia Recreational Atlas*, 5th edition.

8

Introduction

Two years ago when I began to contemplate writing this book I was almost overwhelmed by the enormity of the task. There was so much history and so many cultural and recreational opportunities here that I couldn't imagine how they would fit into one small package. And while I knew how much I have come to love the coast and its people, after living here since 1980, I could not begin to speculate how others felt about it. Nevertheless I plunged in, and as predicted, gathered far more information than I would ever be allowed to use. Everywhere I went people were eager to share with me their stories and their passion for this community. They invited me into their homes, brought me cups of tea, their dusty record books, and faded pictures, or showed me the projects they were working on. Over and over again I found people who had come here, or remained here, because they couldn't bear to live anywhere else. People who had found unique ways to make their living, doing things they enjoyed that also enabled them to stay in the place they loved, and people who had retired here and found themselves busier than when they were employed. They were conducting orchestras, creating breathtaking gardens, joining tennis leagues and canoe clubs ... and loving every minute of what they were doing.

I asked them all why they stayed, what they liked about this Sunshine Coast, and their answers were invariably the same: the incredible scenery with the ocean and islands and mountains, fresh air, peace and nature, the climate that enables year-round gardening, the friendly people, and amazing community spirit. Most of all they valued the slow-paced and informal lifestyle.

Although many grumbled about the cost and inconvenience of the ferry service, equally as many recognized that the lack of an easy way on and off the coast enabled it to maintain a rural atmosphere. The rugged terrain that has discouraged road building to the rest of the lower mainland was also the reason why early European settlers arrived by sea. Consequently there was

One of the many unique shops at Gibsons Landing.

no single beginning that progressed in one direction or another, but several beginnings, many of which occurred at the same time. The result was the development of distinctly different communities, their uniqueness determined by the degree of isolation each settlement experienced. Today these communities, which stretch in ribbon-like fashion from Port Mellon to Earls Cove, continue to retain characteristics that set them apart from each other, even though their feelings about the coast, and their reasons for being here are very much the same.

Closest to the ferry and thus to the city, Langdale is a more urban-oriented community. The homes here are generally newer, with well-cared-for lawns and gardens. Parents are actively involved at the Langdale Elementary School and have consistently come up with innovative ideas for fundraising. While there are several artists and other home-based businesses here, many Langdale residents are employed at the Howe Sound Pulp and Paper Mill, or commute to jobs in Vancouver. Those living near Hopkins and Granthams Landings are mainly retired seniors and summer residents.

The much larger community of Gibsons has a working-class atmosphere that is struggling with the shift from forestry and fishery-related jobs to a more tourist-based economy. At the same time, visitors are fascinated by the daily activities on what many call the "working harbour." This is a community

Earth Day celebrations at Roberts Creek Park.

where outrigger canoes, sailboats, kayaks, fishboats, workboats, and fancy yachts have so far managed to share the same space without pushing each other out of the water.

Roberts Creek is at the same time one of the most laid-back communities on the coast and one of the most intense. As violinist Michelle Bruce put it, "We're allowed to be different in Roberts Creek." Often referring to themselves as "The Nation of Roberts Creek," or "The Gumboot Capital of the World," the community's two flags are a typical Creeker solution to competing popular choices. Here you will find alternative lifestyles, new-age therapies, diets, cultures, and relationships. Here, too, live many of the Sunshine Coast's most vocal environmentalists.

Sechelt is blessed with two cultures existing harmoniously side-by-side. The Sechelt Nation has its own lands, government, and cultural facilities. They are generally a quiet people—unless you happen to attend one of their soccer games!—who are struggling to reconnect with the traditions of their ancestors and integrate them into modern lifestyles.

The non-native community of Sechelt is a conservative collection of people who like to take their time making decisions, trying to ensure they have all the information before they agree to a project. The loss of forest-related jobs is forcing them to look to tourism for employment, but retirees

Halfmoon Bay General Store built by Tommy Beasley in 1938 when the Union Steamships still docked at the Halfmoon Bay wharf. It includes a liquor agency, gift shop, video rentals, and an ice cream stand.

who have come here for the peace and simplicity of small-town living are resisting that move. These same retirees, however, make up a large part of the volunteer force that supports the Festival of the Written Arts and other public events that flood the town with visitors.

It is through the needs of their children that the native and non-native communities have the greatest interaction. Parents and leaders of both groups have joined together to create recreational and educational opportunities that involve sharing schools, playing fields, ice time, and coaches.

There is a wide-ranging population at Halfmoon Bay with one section centred around the community school and another around the summer and retirement homes near the water. Although the settlement originated with people working in the logging camps, it is slowly changing to younger families with high environmental standards. A desire for privacy seems to be paramount with many Halfmoon Bay residents.

Pender Harbour has perhaps the most unique culture of the Sunshine Coast. In some areas, such as Frances Peninsula, the nearest grocery store is still a good thirty minutes away by car. As a consequence, the people here have become self-reliant, purchasing their groceries by the case, and making sure there's extra gas in their tanks before they go home.

Egmont has been the most isolated portion of the Sunshine Coast. Humorously dubbing themselves "Egmonsters," this is a community of fiercely independent individuals who live in one of the most rugged, yet most beautiful environments in the world, on the edge of the Jervis Inlet wilderness and the treacherous whirlpools of the Skookumchuck Rapids.

For many years the population of Pender Harbour and Egmont was limited to a few families who were almost all related. Minding your own business and carrying your own weight were high among both communities' standards. Bad-mouthing a neighbour was definitely not advisable, since you might be talking to that neighbour's cousin. If newcomers followed these rules and turned up to support community projects for 30 or 40 years, there was a good chance that they would be considered a permanent part of the community.

Today with an increasing number of wealthy retirees and summer residents, the atmosphere of Pender Harbour and Egmont is shifting to that of a vacation paradise. Even residents from other parts of the Sunshine Coast flock here during the summer. "Pender Harbour is becoming a playground for the Sunshine Coast," says publisher Howard White. The key to this playland is the recreational opportunities and scenic waterfront that has not yet been developed.

No matter how different each settlement is, within every one of them dwell talented, artistic people who are eager to share what they do best with the rest of the world. In this book I have profiled only a small fraction of a large cultural pie that continuously enriches the Sunshine Coast. In no way does the absence of anyone from these pages signify their lack of importance. There were simply not enough pages to do them justice.

It was a privilege for me to meet with the people who live in my community, to share—for even a brief moment—their stories and passions. They have all helped me to reaffirm what I already knew: the Sunshine Coast is my place to be.

Sechelt Indian Village, 1904.
Newly-built St. Augustine's school in the background.

Sechelt's first hotel was opened by Herbert Whitaker in 1899. The fence
in front was to keep out the sheep. The hotel was destroyed by fire in 1914.
The site was later used for a dance pavilion, movie theatre, and eventually
the Parthenon Restaurant. Today it is the Beach House Residential Complex.

1

Early History

Although it is situated little more than an hour's journey from the city of Vancouver, the Sunshine Coast has a small-town atmosphere. It's a place where high fashion is saved for special occasions, where a trip to the bank can turn into an impromptu visit with friends, and where it's not uncommon to be standing behind a mayor in a supermarket line-up. This laid-back attitude isn't new, for even settlement of this part of the coast was accomplished in a similar unhurried, informal manner.

The first residents are thought to have arrived about a thousand years after the last ice age, roughly around 9,000 or 10,000 B.C.E. This was during the Neolithic Revolution when humans were beginning to cultivate plants and domesticate animals. First Nations' legends tell how their people first came to the Sunshine Coast, but these stories are privately owned by Sechelt Nation families and can only be shared by them. Written history begins when Jose Maria Narvaez made a brief landing at Tsawcome (Wilson Creek) in 1791 to replenish water supplies.

Anthropologists believe that at that time on the Sunshine Coast there were four main groups or septs of the Coast Salish Nations known as the Sechelt or Shishalh, and at least thirty seasonal settlements north of Roberts Creek. Another Coast Salish Nation, the Squamish, occupied the area from Port Mellon to beyond Gibsons.

These early residents lived in longhouses; harvested their food from the sea, the shore, and the land; and made their clothing from cedar bark, mountain goat wool, and the hair of small white dogs. When Captain George Vancouver mapped the Sunshine Coast in the summer of 1792 he noted that the natives of Howe Sound were expert traders, bartering "fish, their garments, spears, bows and arrows ... [and] copper ornaments." Because the natives did not understand English, Spanish, or Nootka, he was forced to use sign language to communicate with them.

*Three totem poles await unveiling on the Sechelt Indian Band waterfront.
The poles complete a quintet recognizing and honouring the four septs
that make up the Sechelt Nation as well as milestones in the Shishalh's struggle
to achieve self-government and the settlement of their land claims.
From left to right the poles honour the* tewankw, *the* ts'únay,
the shishálh *people, the* sxixus, *and the* xénichén.

The first major interaction between the Shishalhs and Europeans occurred in 1860 when Father Leon Fouquet of the Oblate Order of Mary Immaculate came to convert the people of Pender Harbour. He was not welcomed and within two months was forced to leave; however, when the smallpox epidemic of 1862 reduced their population from five thousand people to less than two hundred, the Shishalh changed their minds. Worn down by illness and the horror of watching their families and leaders suffer the agonies of smallpox and die, and believing that the epidemic was caused by their rejection of the priest, the survivors sent two chiefs to the Oblates' St. Charles Mission in New Westminster to ask the priests to return.

Father Paul Durieu agreed to the chiefs' request and used the opportunity to create what he saw as a model native Christian community. His first step was to gather all of the tribes together in one area, which he named Sechelt, abolish the traditional chieftainships, and appoint four new "chiefs" and a number of "watchmen" and "soldiers" who policed the village and dealt out penances and punishment. Gambling, potlatches, dancing, and shamanism were also forbidden. While they appeared to obey the missionaries and the new European laws, in secret the Sechelts continued to hold potlatches and other traditional ceremonies, and to acknowledge their traditional chiefs.

As Durieu worked to build his model community, steps were underway in the rest of the colony to form a union with Canada, and in July 1871 the province of British Columbia was established. By this time Sewell Moody of the Moodyville Sawmill was beginning to log timber on land that the Sechelts claimed as their own; so, in 1873 an armed confrontation occurred between the Sechelts and Jabez A. Culver, a pre-emptor who was cutting spars for Moody on the site of the former Tewankw settlement in Narrows Inlet. Culver and his men left, but the government in Victoria sent the man-of-war H.M.S. *Myrmidon* to Trail Bay with the superintendent of police and Magistrate Bushby on board. Under this threat, the Sechelts agreed to allow Culver and other handloggers to return, and Bushby promised that their land claims would receive attention. Like most promises surrounding land claims, this one was broken.

On July 17, 1875 John Scales, a stonemason with the corps of British Royal Engineers, received as a free military land grant a 150-acre parcel of land bordering what is now Trail Bay, along with an additional 110 acres on Porpoise Bay. Although Scales never actually lived on this land, his grant marked the beginning of European settlement on the Sunshine Coast. Five years later a widowed Scottish-Portuguese fisherman named Joseph Silvia Simmonds, who eventually became known as Joseph Silvey, married a Sechelt woman, Lucy Kwatleematt, and moved to Egmont with his two Musqueam daughters. Many of their descendants still live in the area.

Over the next ten years great changes took place in British Columbia, especially after the railroad joining east to west was completed and Vancouver became a terminus for passenger ships from the Orient. As the lower mainland developed, settlers and loggers were drawn to new wilderness areas like the Sunshine Coast where pre-emptions were still available and timber grew close to the water, making it easy to harvest and transport to market. Many stayed only long enough to remove the timber from their pre-emptions, then abandoned them. Other men, such as George Gibson Sr., persevered through isolation, food shortages, disease, and fire to establish permanent homes.

George Gibson grew up in Queen Victoria's England, a time when the nation was changing from an agricultural to an industrial economy. Even shipbuilding was affected, and when George joined the British navy in 1839 that institution was already shifting from sailing schooners to ships driven with steam-powered propellers. Only three years earlier the *Beaver* had become the first steamboat to arrive at Fort Vancouver.

George left the navy in 1856 and set off for America where he spent three years working on the Great Lakes. In 1859, shortly after the end of the Civil War, he married Augusta "Charlotte" Purdy, daughter of an American trader. They settled in Chatham, Ontario, where George became a successful market gardener.

Statue of George Gibson, sculpted by the late Jack Harman, who was considered one of the top sculptors in North America. The statue faces the sea and is located in Pioneer Park just below the Gibson family cemetery. Across the street from the park is the home that Dr. Fred Inglis built in 1912.

In his late fifties, George embarked on a new adventure. With his two sons, 25-year-old George Jr. and eighteen-year-old Ralph, he left Ontario, travelled by train to San Francisco and boarded a ship bound for Victoria. After finding temporary employment in Nanaimo, the three men built an eighteen-foot sloop, the *Swamp Angel*. They hoped to travel to Lulu Island to pre-empt farm land, but on a trial voyage they were blown off course across Georgia Strait to the southern shore of Keats Island. They made camp for the night and in the morning discovered that the island was only a short distance from a wild, unsettled shore that proved to be part of the mainland. This, they decided, was the land they wanted to pre-empt and according to his granddaughter, Hazel Wood, George never regretted his decision. "The whole family just seemed to think that's the place where they should be."

Although local and family records indicate that George and his sons staked their claim in 1886, the date of their application in Volume 99 of the New Westminster Pre-emption Register is May 2, 1887. It is possible that before registering the land, the Gibson men went on to Lulu Island to work for Dan Woodward, and from there to Vancouver where it is known that George Sr. was hired to build the wharf at the foot of Carrall Street, which was later used by the Union Steamship Company. He also served for a short time on the newly formed Vancouver City Council. His wife and younger daughters joined him in August 1886 and a year later they moved to their pre-emption.

The Gibsons' daughter Mary Ann and her husband W. George Glassford soon followed her parents west. George, however, was not enthusiastic about the new province. His granddaughter Pearle Tretheway remembers him saying, "If I'd had the money, I'd have gone right back. It was pouring rain and all those big trees!"

The Glassfords registered their claim on the same day as George Gibson. By 1887, having tired of living in the tent city of Vancouver, they moved with their friends, the James Fletcher family, to Howe Sound. George Gibson Sr. invited the two families to build temporary housing on his homestead while they cleared and developed their own property. Two years later the Glassford's daughter Grace became the first non-native child to be born in the community.

The Gibsons family: Photo taken around 1890. Back Row: Minister Lacy, unknown, Charlotte Gibson, Ralph Gibson, Chuck Winegarden, Lloyd Baker, George Gibson, Sr., unknown, Emma Gibson, Charlotte Gibson Sr. Front row: Tom Soames, Mary Lusk, Harriet Gibson, Tom Andrew Jr., Irene Smith, Nellie Gibson, Sadie Soames, and Eliza Andrew.

Charlotte Gibson

Born in Michigan in 1839, Augusta Charlotte Purdy spent much of her childhood travelling back and forth on the Oregon Trail with her wagon master father. During these years she learned the basics of nursing and midwifery from her mother. When she was nineteen Charlotte married George Gibson in Sebewaine, Michigan, and moved to Chatham, Ontario.

In 1885, just four years after their eighth child was born, George and their two sons abandoned the comforts of civilization for the adventure of homesteading along the west coast. A year later Charlotte packed their belongings and with her four youngest daughters, boarded one of the first trains to Port Moody. From there they took the side-wheeler *Princess Louisa* across Indian Arm to the tent city built on the remnants of the 1886 fire that had destroyed Vancouver. After living for a short time in Vancouver, the family moved into the two-storey frame house George had built on the hillside of their new homestead at Howe Sound, just behind what is now Molly's Reach.

Charlotte's life in this new land began with a tragedy when in July 1888 her eldest daughter, Eliza Andrews, died of a heart condition caused by rheumatic fever. Eliza and her husband Thomas had pre-empted land close to the Gibson's homestead, but at the time of her death were staying in Vancouver where Thomas was a night watchman.

It's possible that Charlotte feared a second tragedy one Christmas day as she waited anxiously for George to return from Vancouver with much-needed supplies. A snowstorm swept over the settlement, reducing visibility on the water to zero and it was ten o'clock in the evening before the tug, *Vancouver*, pulled up to the wharf long enough to drop off a side of beef and the message that George was coming. It was after midnight before he made it home.

Charlotte soon became the person all of the Howe Sound settlers went to when they were sick or when a baby was due. Even the local Squamish people, who nicknamed her "The Swamp Angel" after her husband's boat, would come to her for help when they were sick. She would go with them in their canoes, and sometimes be gone for as long as a week. It is said that she always welcomed unexpected guests and provided them with a warm drink and nourishment. In 1892 when Arthur Hyde was dying of smallpox, Charlotte didn't hesitate to take him in and nurse him. Two weeks after his death her own children came down with the disease. Fortunately, they all recovered.

When Charlotte died of Bright's disease in May 1910 at the age of 72, many of her children and grandchildren were living near her home. On her tombstone, which still stands in Pioneer Park is the inscription, "She rests from her labors and her works do follow."

The Gibson, Glassford, and Fletcher families were soon joined by other pioneers: the Hydes, Paynes, Soames, and Pratts—names that can now be found on streets that run close to where their homesteads used to be. The new settlement, known first as West Howe Sound, then as Gibson's Landing in 1906, and finally as Gibsons (without the apostrophe) in 1947, would eventually become the second largest municipality on the Sunshine Coast.

Two years after the arrival of the Gibson clan another English immigrant, Thomas William "Will" Roberts, pre-empted land bordering the creek that now bears his name. Within a year he had proved up his homestead and promptly sold it to his parents, Thomas and Charlotte Roberts. The former head gardener of a huge estate in England, Thomas developed the orchard Will had started and planted a garden. Many of the foxgloves that grow wild along the banks of the creek are said to have originated from his plants. The couple was friendly with many of the Sechelt people who referred to the waterway as "Fat Fish Creek"[1] and to Thomas as "the Big King George Man," possibly because of his height and long beard.

A year after their arrival, the Roberts were joined by their daughter Alice and her husband William Henry "Dan" Steinbrunner who pre-empted 160 acres at what is now the corner of Lockyer Road and Highway 101. Dan cleared and planted his own garden and orchard and constructed a barn. Within only a few years the Steinbrunner farm had hayfields, cattle, pigs, and chickens— and three babies: Tom, Herb, and Ruby.

It's possible that in June of 1890 both the Roberts and the Gibson families paused from their labours long enough to participate in a Sechelt celebration for the opening of Our Lady of the Rosary church. More than a thousand natives arrived on the steamer *Yosemite*, among them five brass bands that joined the Sechelts' own brass ensemble. Twice the *Yosemite* returned, her decks filled with excursionists from Vancouver who came to take part in festivities that included fireworks and a parade of canoes from the Squamish Nation.

In August 1891, perhaps lured by the publicity surrounding the Sechelt Festival, Thomas Cook, a Canadian Pacific Railway steward, homesteaded on land between what is now Shornecliff and St. Hilda's Church. A year later Alfred Whitaker and his seventeen-year-old son Herbert "Bert" pre-empted property on the west side of Porpoise Bay, and by 1894 both the Cook and Whitaker families had established residences in the area. The following year Bert purchased the original Scales property and began subdividing and promoting what he called "Seechelt Township," eventually establishing a small empire of stores, a steamship company, wharves, sawmills, and logging camps.

Harry Roberts' "castle" was built at Roberts Creek in 1917. This photo shows the castle, slightly renovated, but still in use, 82 years after it was built.

Harry Roberts looking at trees; some were eleven and twelve feet in diameter. c. 1910.

A Walk in the Woods with Harry Roberts

Harry Roberts was only sixteen when he helped his father row the 25 miles from False Creek to his grandparents' old homestead at Roberts Creek. Shortly after they had settled in he made his first trip to Gibsons along a little-used trail of interlinking skid roads.

"This old skid road was like a tunnel with little windows to let the light come down to the path, which was a box a foot or so wide between young alders," he wrote in a 1964 *Coast News* article describing the journey. Having frequently sketched the old bridges near his English home, he was curious about the first one he encountered. "[The material] had all been taken from the woods right there. All was of red cedar. The deck was split pieces almost two feet wide by half a foot thick and about a dozen feet long–a real bit of good strong handiwork! Not a bit of iron in the whole structure, just a few wooden pins."

Some of the forest resembled English parkland. Harry was awed by the stillness and compared the setting to an old church. "The hushed feeling was the same, but there was an intense loneliness. Though farther back I had hoped I wouldn't meet a bear, now the sight of one, far enough away, would have been welcome. Yes, I'd have been very glad to see even a little English sparrow."

When Harry finally reached a hill overlooking the Gibsons harbour, he yearned for his paints and the time to capture the scene below him for his old art master. "A background of mighty stalwart mountains was silhouetted against a clear sky. Bowen Island and a smaller one (Keats) stood out with every detail, in the water, as clear as above it. The foreground of boats and logs, then the different greens which came towards me up the hill."

Unfortunately, Harry was far too busy to capture anything on canvas. Working with his father and Uncle Dan Steinbrunner, he did everything from clearing land to salting fish, and during the winter he apprenticed at Wallace's Shipyards in False Creek. As an adult his artistic nature was expressed in building boats such as the *Chack Chack*—a 36-foot yawl with an eagle carved on the prow—and unusual houses, such as the "Castle," which can be seen from the beach at Roberts Creek, and "Sunray," a building on Nelson Island that is still being used as a summer residence by descendants of the island's pioneers. Harry also wrote two books, *The Natural Laws* and *The Trail of Chack Chack*.

His Trail Bay waterfront operations, including a hotel, general store, post office, and dance hall, became the core of the fledgling community.

At the northern end of the Sunshine Coast, the European settlement initiated by Joseph Silvey had expanded and by 1891 Union Steamship excursion boats were bringing the first tourists to a store-cum-post office and hotel owned by Charles Irvine in the area known as Irvines Landing. His holdings were sold in 1904 to a former sailor and fisherman from the Madeira Islands, Joe Gonsalves. After a family quarrel, Joes set out in his early teens to see the world, stowing aboard a ship that took him around South America to Guyana where he had to disembark with smallpox. A year later he travelled to San Francisco, then to Vancouver. There he married Susan Harris of the North Vancouver Salish Nation.

After purchasing Charles Irvine's property for six dollars an acre, Joe, Susan, their five daughters, and son Alfred moved to Irvines Landing. Across the bay Joe also obtained a 160-acre pre-emption that he called his "farm." Many years later his daughter Theresa named the community situated on the site of his homestead "Madeira Park" after her father's homeland.

The Gonsalve's daughter Matilda married a Russian seaman named Theodore Dames who became Joe's partner in building a larger hotel and a saloon at the head of the Irvines Landing wharf. Theirs was the only store in Pender Harbour until 1914 when Robert Donley, a one-armed Detroit steam engineer, opened a store and established a fish-buying business at Donley's Landing—located at what is now the foot of Hassan Road.

Although all of the Sunshine Coast was isolated because of the lack of roads to the rest of the mainland, Pender Harbour was further isolated because for many years there was no road connecting it to Sechelt, Roberts Creek, or Gibsons. Nor were there roads connecting the tiny settlements that existed beside the numerous coves and bays that made up the shorelines of Egmont and Pender Harbour.

"We never went anywhere," said Cledia Duncan (née Warnock) in an oral history taped for the Elphinstone Pioneer Museum. "My dad used to take us to Vancouver once in a while, that was all. You could go by Union Steamship down to Halfmoon Bay ... but we never went on the steamer."

As a consequence of the isolation, the people here were more close-knit and self-reliant than elsewhere and many of the older families intermarried— the Jeffries, Gonsalves, Dames, Warnocks, Duncans, Reids, and Wrays—to name only a few. This kinship didn't, however, stop them from playing tricks on each other. In his own oral history, Wilfred "Tiffy" Wray remembers a Halloween prank he and his friends played on Joe Gonsalves:

Smallpox

By the end of the 1862 smallpox epidemic, which reduced the native population on the Sunshine Coast to less than two hundred people, most of the survivors had developed a natural immunity to the disease or had been vaccinated against it. Some people, however, including the new settlers arriving in the late 1880s, were more afraid of the vaccine than the disease.

In Vancouver in the spring of 1892, the *Empress of Japan* brought a number of passengers from China who had smallpox. One of the ship's pursers, Arthur Hyde, was placed in charge of these passengers during their quarantine. Unaware that he too had been infected, Hyde returned to his homestead at Howe Sound. When he became ill, he went to Charlotte Gibson for help and although she took him into her home and nursed him as best she could, his smallpox was too far advanced and he died a short time later. By then the Gibson family had contracted the disease.

"They all got it except Uncle Ralph," says the Gibson's granddaughter, Hazel Wood. "He lived next door. Every day he'd come to the fence and talk to my grandfather to see how the family was, but he didn't dare come in."

Hazel's mother, seventeen-year-old Charlotte "Lottie" Gibson, was the first to fall ill. "My mother was so low that they expected her to die. They had her coffin waiting on the wharf ... Her hair was shaved off. It had been so curly and thick it used to tangle and she hoped it would come back straight, but it came back curlier than ever."

Arthur Hyde was the only fatality of the epidemic, which infected a total of eleven people. The Gibson home became the quarantine centre where Sisters Francis and Jesse from St. James Anglican Church in Vancouver nursed patients. The steamer *Sunberry* called in daily with fresh meat or provisions.

In the *Gibson's Landing Story*, Lester R. Peterson tells of how this outbreak led to the desertion of the Chek-Welp Indian village:

"Years later, Fred Soames related, a canoe with a single paddler made its way down the Sound. As it passed by the Soames property, the lone traveler called out, asking if the epidemic was over.

The answer was yes."

"We took a bunch of old corn stalks and put them on the hotel verandah and somebody got a couple of dog fish and threw them in. The next morning, of course, Mr. Gonsalves complained, so the policeman came to have a look. His remark was, it must have been an awful high tide last night."

Ethnic Settlement

While most of the new settlements on the Sunshine Coast were predominately Anglo, there were many ethnic communities as well. Perhaps the earliest were the Chinese labourers who worked in the shingle mill at Clowhom from 1906 to 1931 and in the early logging operations elsewhere along the coast. It is rumoured that Charles Irvine purchased his Pender Harbour holdings around 1886 from a Chinese trader, although there are no pre-emption records available to prove or disprove the story. Most Chinese settlements were little more than shantytowns where men worked long hard hours for a pittance and a dream of a better way of life. These towns and the men disappeared when the mills or logging operations closed down, but they left behind a treasure trove of ceramic jars and tiny opium bottles for dedicated collectors to find.

Japanese immigrants stayed longer and established permanent homes in Pender Harbour and Sechelt. Many of Sechelt's early pioneers feasted on fruits and vegetables from Jiro "Jim" Konishi's farm on the west shore of Porpoise Bay. A Japanese-Canadian fish buyer named Nakashima owned the first store in Egmont. Two other fish buyers were the Takais and Maedas. A cabinetmaker called Kahara carved a beautiful maple leaf above the front entrance to the Maple Leaf School in Egmont.

In her oral history Lewella Duncan remembers the cod fisherman Ikeda's family. "One of the girls was a very close friend of mine, and the Harbour loved the Ikedas."

The Japanese settlements disappeared during the Second World War when the government confiscated the settlers' boats and houses and sent them off to internment camps. Says Llewella, "Everybody in the Harbour went over to the steam boat when they took the Ikedas away and everybody was crying. It was just terrible. They [the government] claimed their boats, I think they took them up to Steveston or something, and I know they went to the camp in the interior and my friend Bessie Ikeda she lost a baby there ... It was a terrible blow for the Pender Harbour people. Not just to our family."

Another Pender Harbour community, known as Hardscratch, was settled by Scottish immigrants. Robert McKay, whose parents purchased property there in 1918 remembers in his oral history that, "The Scots were very cliquish. My grandfather, my uncles, and my aunts were all congregated in one little area and of course they spoke the Scottish tongue." He also told of the Scots bachelors who would often come to dinner uninvited. "There were about 40 or so. They lived in these little boats. By, God, they would tie to your float, or anchor the boat in front of your house and they were always around at mealtime. Every family had one … Like my brother-in-law. There was twelve of them in that family, and a guy that anchored in front of their house came for every meal. And you know, it was hard for them to put a meal on the table. There was always more water in the soup."

In 1905 a Finnish settlement was established in Gibsons. Disillusioned with a communal society on Malcolm Island, Karl Wiren, Jack Hintsa, Andy Wilander, and the Ruise family purchased homesteads along what are now Cemetery, Payne, and Henry Roads.

By1910 there were sixteen Finnish families living in upper Gibsons. Most of these new settlers were farmers, like Karl Wiren who raised a dairy herd and established a milk delivery service.

Among the Finlanders' contributions to the settlement was the building of two community halls. The first, located at the corner of Sechelt Highway and Payne Road on land donated by John Wiren, was built under the leadership of Jake Hintsa and became known as the Socialist Hall. Here they held dances, fall fairs, and meetings of the newly formed Farmer's Institute—a 30-member group established in 1911 to enable local farmers to purchase stumping powder at a lower rate than individuals. The second hall, constructed because of a conflict in the philosophical views of various members of the community, was located on land donated by Mr. Ruise, just west of Payne Creek. It was called The Workers Hall and most events held there were conducted in the Finnish language. Many descendants of these early Finnish pioneers still live on the Sunshine Coast.

Another Scandinavian group were the Swedish loggers who operated or worked in logging camps along Jervis and Salmon Inlet during the 1920s and 1930s where only Swedes were hired and only Swedish was spoken. Harold Swanson, who came to work in the camps in his early teens, claimed it was years before he discovered there were men of other nationalities out in the woods. Many of these immigrant loggers, like the Gustavsons and Swansons, stayed to settle on the Sunshine Coast permanently.

The most recent group of settlers to the Coast came in the 1960s and 1970s. While not ethnically similar—although many were Americans—they were known as "hippies," "war protesters," and "back-to-the-landers." Arriving with little money and often even less skills, they established communes on forestry land along the inlets or on the abandoned properties of the early

The Gower Point Fire

In August 1906, just four months after the great San Francisco earthquake, the settlement of Gibson's Landing was ravaged by fire. It began when the newly settled Madden family decided to burn a pile of brush on their property at the north end of what is now Leek Road. Without considering the tinder-dry condition of the neighbouring forest or the strong westerly wind that was blowing, they started a small fire that quickly spread along the ground into nearby brush. Soon it reached the woods where it was beyond anyone's control.

"The treetops were a solid mass of flame," Fire Warden McKay was quoted as saying by the August 24, 1906 *Province* newspaper. "I never saw anything like the fury of the burning blaze in my life before. Burning brands were thrown fully two thousand feet by the wind. The smoke arising was exceptionally dense."

While some ranchers were able to bury precious items in their yards, most were forced to flee the flames, leaving everything behind. One Finnish woman was giving birth as the fire was closing in on her home. As soon as the baby was born, mother and child were moved by stretcher to the wharf where a crowd of women and children were sheltering from the smoke.

When the fire finally burned itself out, one person was dead and more than $50,000 worth of equipment, buildings, bridges, and timber had been destroyed from Leek Road to Langdale Creek, including the flume owned by the logging company of Battle and Drew on Mount Elphinstone.

loggers and homesteaders. Peter Light, one of the few who have maintained this freedom-loving lifestyle, related, "With my four-week-old daughter, a three-month supply of groceries, and some tools I moved up to Storm Bay. On the way I flipped my last dime into Porpoise Bay. It's probably still there."

Few of the communes lasted for long, but in Roberts Creek many of the more enduring hippies established permanent roots and helped to create one of the most unique communities on the Sunshine Coast—known fondly as "The Gumboot Capital of the World." Here you will find the annual Earth Day celebrations and the crowning of *Mr.* Roberts Creek, which is a favourite part of their annual Creek Daze festival.

Government History

As migrations to the Sunshine Coast increased, local governments were formed with Gibsons pioneering the move by incorporating as the Village of Gibson's Landing on March 4, 1929. William W. Winn, Flora Jack, and Sidney Holland signed the application. At that time the village encompassed 290 acres, including George Gibson's original pre-emption.

William Winn was elected as the first chairman, while George Cooper and J.J. Corlett were elected as commissioners. These latter two men retained their positions for the next 21 years, mostly because other qualified candidates were scarce and because Cooper and Corlett adhered strictly to the citizens' demand that there be no increase in land taxes. As village clerk Robert "Bob" Burns said in a 1955 speech, "We opened up every lane in the village so they could be traveled by autos, got a water system, a fire department handcart and hose, bought the water springs property, and later installed a gravity line with a good supply of water for all who wanted it. We did all those things without increasing taxes."

Sechelt's first Mayor, Christine Johnson.

The municipality's name was changed in 1950 to the Village of Gibsons (the boundaries having been extended to include George Gibson Jr.'s pre-emption) and again in 1983 to the Town of Gibsons. In 1998 the estimated population of the town was 3,926 residents and its land area contained 4.24 square kilometres running roughly from Mahan and Payne Roads north to Reed Road, east to Checkwelp Indian Reserve, and south to the Strait of Georgia.

A 1948 survey of Sechelt residents showed that 55 percent were in favour of incorporation. The same percentage won a plebiscite on the subject eight years later when Ted Osborne, Steve Howlett, and Ernie Parr Pearson were appointed interim commissioners of the 513-acre village, formally established on February 15, 1956. At that time it contained four hundred residents. Within two months Christine Johnson, Hugh Bernel Gordon, Captain Sam Dawe, Alec Lamb, and Frank Parker were elected to the first village council. Christine Johnston became the first chairman (mayor). The wife of local magistrate Captain Andrew Johnston and owner of a variety and jewellery store, Christine had grown up with politics. One of her childhood memories was of walks in an Ottawa park with former Prime Minister, Sir Wilfred Laurier, who always had a peppermint in his pocket for her.

Although he had opposed incorporation, Hugh Bernel Gordon received the second highest number of votes. As a *Coast News* reporter observed about the election: "The women will be happy because one of their sex was elected and opponents to incorporation will be happy because their stalwart was elected. The other three will no doubt satisfy the remainder of the electorate."[2]

In 1990 the village of Sechelt became a town as the boundaries were expanded to include Sandy Hook, Tuwanek, Selma Park, and Davis Bay and by 1996 the population had increased to 7,343 residents.

Administration and welfare of the Indians of British Columbia was transferred in 1871 to the federal government under the Department of Indian Affairs. On February 11, 1925 the four tribes that spoke the Shishahl language— the Sqaia-quos of Pender Harbour, the Tsonai of Deserted Bay, the Klam-am-klatc at the head of Jervis Inlet, and the Tahw-ahn-kwuh at the head of Narrows Inlet—officially amalgamated to form the Sechelt Indian Band.

Denied the right to vote in federal, provincial, or municipal elections, the Sechelt Indian Band at this time was governed by an Indian Agent who met infrequently with an informal council of hereditary chiefs from the four main tribes. These meetings were not encouraged by the government, nor were they very effective. It was not until 1953 that a new Indian Act enabled members of the Sechelt Indian Band to choose their own leader. On January 14, 1953, Charles Craigan became their first elected chief.

In 1971, led by Chief Henry Paul, and later by Chief Stanley Dixon, the Sechelt Indian Band began petitioning Ottawa for self-government. This was a long and often frustrating process that ended in 1986 when the Sechelt Self Government Act established the Sechelt Indian Band as an independent, autonomous, corporate body and paved the way for the Sechelt Indian Band Council to govern the band's affairs. The band elects the chief and council members for three-year terms.

Today, with a population of 1,030 members, the band is negotiating with federal and provincial governments to settle their land claims treaty. In 1999 they signed an agreement-in-principal with the federal and provincial governments, earning the honour of being the band first to reach such an agreement under the B.C. Treaty Commission. Unfortunately, that agreement fell apart and the band is once again exploring both political and legal avenues to settle their land claims.

Rural areas of the Sunshine Coast are governed by the Sunshine Coast Regional District (SCRD), an organization that began with provincial legislation passed in 1965 that amalgamated over three hundred improvement districts into administrated areas designated by the provincial government. In 1967 Cliff Gilker and Frank West, who had already been involved in efforts to establish rural water and garbage services, were two of the six local

The Gumboot Garden Café

The business district of Roberts Creek is known by many as the "heart of the Creek," and the Gumboot Garden Café as the heart of that "heart." Built as a trading post in 1926 by a Mr. Gillman, the property was sold a year later and the buildings became the H. Robinson General Store. The post office was added in 1931 and twelve years later the Robinsons' son-in-law Ted Shaw took over the business. When he retired in 1958 the post office was moved to a new building beside the Seaview Market; the store was closed until the late 1960s when a co-operative of newly arrived hippies reopened it as a wholesale outlet, barbershop, ice cream parlour, and upstairs, a speak-easy. The manager, a Las Vegas dancer who insists she be known only as "Nancye," kept the club peaceful. "If anybody got drunk, I'd lock them up and call their old lady," she boasted. "I encouraged women to dress up, come out, and show respect." After Nancye left, the speak-easy wasn't the same. "I gave it over to some people from town and they didn't last long. They wrecked the house. That's when it got called The Goon Saloon, 'cause goons was running it."

In the mid-1990s a company called Heart Of The Creek purchased the property. Laurie O'Byrne, one of the shareholders and co-owner of the café, is a dedicated Creeker. "There's a strong community here," she says seriously. "It's like my 80-year-old neighbour said: 'People are there for you if you need them. Otherwise they mind their own business.'"

Truly appreciating the flavour of the Gumboot Café involves sitting back and watching the ebb and flow of people, many with children in tow, greeting each other as good friends, sharing a meal or a veggie drink, stopping to view the latest addition to the informal gallery of artwork, listening in the evening to music or political debate. For strangers it's like stepping back 30 years to an era of long hair, flowing skirts, startling footwear, sitar music, and brotherhood. For Creekers, it's just another place where they can be.

citizens elected to the SCRD's first board of directors. Gradually all of the water works on the Sunshine Coast came under SCRD control, as well as regional and community planning, contract services for incorporated members, local works and services, refuse disposal, and the creation and maintenance of many of the parks and recreation services available here.

The SCRD is divided into six alphabetical areas, each with an elected representative who serves on a Board of Directors. Also on the Board are representatives from the Gibsons, Sechelt, and Sechelt Indian Band councils.

Pender Harbour falls within the scope of Area A, which extends from Wood Bay north to Egmont and includes Jervis Inlet and Hardy and Nelson Islands. In the fall of 1999 a referendum was held to decide if the area was to form a separate municipality at the north end of the Sunshine Coast. Those in favour of incorporating wanted more say in local decisions, while those opposed felt that the tax base was too small to support a municipality. A 55 percent majority defeated the referendum.

Area B, also known as Halfmoon Bay, includes Welcome Beach, Sargeant's Bay, and Smuggler's Cove. Covering Salmon and Narrows Inlet, Area C is a sparsely populated district that includes sections along the highway on the west side of Sechelt and between Sechelt and Roberts Creek, while Area D covers Roberts Creek itself. Area E runs between Roberts Creek and Gibsons, and Area F encompasses the West Howe Sound area, including Langdale and Port Mellon.

Although Nelson Island falls under the jurisdiction of the SCRD as a part of Area A, Gambier and Keats Islands are governed both by the SCRD and the Islands Trust and are represented by a local committee with one member appointed from the Islands Trust and two elected members. Islands Trust is responsible for planning and development applications, while services are provided by the SCRD. Generally these services are limited. There is no garbage collection, street lighting, or car ferry, and the few roads that exist are unnamed and unpaved.

The Gambier Island Conservancy was organized in 1995 to counteract the increasing development pressures facing the island from new subdivision development, potential commercial logging and pressure for recreational use of its crown land. Much of their work focuses on biophysical inventories, stream assessments and rehabilitation, and a geographical information system. Among their findings are trees that are 1,300 years old. Close working relationships have been formed between the Conservancy, the Ministry of Environment, Lands and Parks, Islands Trust, SCRD, and Capilano College.

Also under the care of the Islands Trust are Pasley, Merry, Anvil, and Boyer Islands. The Shelter Islands, between Gibsons and Keats Island, are owned and governed by the Squamish Indian Band.

2

A Place to Work

Forestry-Related Work

Traditionally the First Nations people of the Sunshine Coast lived off the land and water, but with the arrival of the Europeans, the Sechelts' self-sufficiency was gradually eroded by disease, alcohol, and the restrictive laws of the federal and provincial governments. Although no treaties were ever signed, the native people were forced onto reserves and denied the right to purchase or pre-empt land as the new settlers were doing. For a while they could earn their living handlogging, but in 1908 the provincial government passed a law whereby only persons named on the provincial voters' list could stake handlogging claims. Since the native people had already been disenfranchised in 1871, the new regulation also excluded them. Adapting once more to laws they couldn't change, the Sechelts began working for non-native handlogging and gyppo outfits, their jobs ranging from skid greaser and chokerman to high rigger and sawyer.

Handlogging was useful in areas where timber could be easily rolled to the water and didn't need to be hauled. Although hard and dangerous, this type of logging required little capital expenditure and therefore provided a livelihood for many early settlers such as Donald and John McNaughton, Jimmy Archibald, and Herman Solberg. Larger shows with horses, oxen, rollways, and flumes were successful in harvesting timber from further inland. They were run by men such as Robert McNair, J. McMyn, and John Klein. Donkey engines were introduced at the beginning of the twentieth century as was railroad logging. The Heaps Timber Company established a railroad show at Narrows Inlet in 1907, and P.B. Anderson & Company ran one at Pender Harbour from 1912 to 1916. Eric and Thure Gustavson ran a railroad show at Salmon Inlet's Gustavson Bay in the early 1930s. Truck logging was being carried out at Oscar Niemi's Halfmoon Bay Logging Company camp around

Big Douglas fir being felled, Roberts Creek or Wilson Creek area,
Burns and Jackson Logging. Two men on springboards, one on either
side of a tree, while a small boy sits in the cut. c. 1937.

1927, and Brown and Kirkland (B & K) Logging had a truck camp at Sechelt Creek in the early 1930s that they moved to Roberts Creek in 1937.

By 1950, the annual timber cut on the Sunshine Coast was 35 million board feet, and statistics gathered three years later showed that approximately 2,000 acres were being clearcut in the Sechelt Forest District every year. As early as the end of the 1970s alarm bells were ringing in forestry circles over the decrease in accessible timber. In 1999 the annual allowable cut for the Sunshine Coast, which now included the Powell Forest District, was 1,140,000 cubic meters.

Modern harvesting methods and the depleted forest resources have resulted in fewer timber-related jobs. In the 1980s Weldwood's Clowhom logging operation was running a 90-man camp complete with a cookhouse and eight bunkhouses. Twenty years later International Forest Products (Interfor) is operating both Clowhom and their Vancouver Bay camp with a crew of 40 men who alternate between the two areas, commuting by boat from their Sunshine Coast homes each day.

Shingle Mill at Clowhom Falls, 1931.

Still, forestry continues to be a primary industry on the coast. In 2000 there were logging operations in West Sechelt, Sechelt Inlet, Salmon Inlet, Howe Sound, Pender Harbour, Egmont, and Jervis Inlet. Approximately fifteen log salvage operators, or beachcombers, were also working on the coast at the end of that year.

Many Sunshine Coast people have found other unique ways to continue earning their living from the forest. Guy Foster, of Amblepark Nurseries, started a Christmas tree forest in 1984, marketing up to 2,300 trees per season. He offers a selection of cut trees, and a small forest where people can choose to cut their own. Lance and Monika Grey run Selma Park Evergreens, a renewable forest industry started in 1970 by her parents, Don and Monty Shinn, that supplies florists with everything from cedar boughs to ferns, salal, and huckleberry branches.

Although there was a shingle mill at Clowhom Falls as early as 1906, the first major sawmill to operate on the Sunshine Coast was opened on the east side of Porpoise Bay in 1948 by the B.C. Fir Company. Today the largest sawmill on the coast is a family-owned business, Bayside Sawmills Ltd. Employing 125 people, the company's specialty lumber products are shipped to Canadian, Japanese, United States, European, and Asian markets.

The biggest employer on the Sunshine Coast, the Howe Sound Pulp and Paper Mill at Port Mellon, was the first mill to make paper out of wood fibre in the province. Started in 1909 by Captain Henry A. Mellon of Vancouver under the name "Pioneer Mills," the original mill produced a good grade of wrapping paper. Unfortunately, the coal-fuelled operation was too costly, and only four months after it opened the plant was closed down. Converted to the kraft process by the Rainy River Pulp & Paper Company in 1917, the mill began using local second-growth logs that were hauled to a landing by horse teams or brought by water into a slough beside the river mouth. The plant was operated with 65 workers on two shifts: an eleven-hour day shift and a thirteen-hour night shift with no spare workers, so that if one operator was ill his opposite number worked 24 hours without relief. Two years later this company went into bankruptcy and the mill was closed once more.

Today Canadian Forest Products Ltd. (Canfor) and Oji Paper of Japan own equal shares in the 52-hectare complex that employs 600 people, has a $40 million payroll, and produces 1,000 tonnes of pulp and 600 tonnes of newsprint each day. In the past ten years they have installed proven environmental systems costing over 120 million dollars. "We buy over ten million dollars of local goods and services each year," says Community Relations Assistant Pamela Kaatz. "Through payroll deductions, our employees donate over $23,000 annually to local charities, and corporately Howe Sound Pulp and Paper contributes to numerous service groups, community organizations, and events." A tour of the Port Mellon plant can be arranged by calling 604-885-4493, local 575.

Fisheries-Related Work

In the same way that provincial laws kept the Sechelt people from obtaining logging claims, federal fisheries regulations also denied them the right to fish commercially. They could only stand by and watch as the new settlers to the coast filled their boats with salmon and cod and delivered them to fish buyers such as Herbert Whitaker at Sechelt and Robert Donley of Pender Harbour, and to canneries that were established in Pender Harbour and Jervis Inlet. When a change to the fishing regulations in 1923 finally enabled the Sechelt people to sell their fish, the abundant catches they had once enjoyed at their doorstep were gone, and they had to travel to the central coast to fish and work for the canneries at Rivers Inlet.

Boat used by the late Hubert Evans to handline for salmon off Salmon Rock in Gibson's during the 1930s. On display at the Elphinstone Pioneer Museum.

This was not, however, the end of fishing along the Sunshine Coast. In the 1930s Bertrand "Bill" Sinclair wrote of purse seiners fishing off Lasqueti Island, pulling in hauls that ranged from 1,000 to 5,000 salmon. Gillnetters fished Jervis Inlet whenever there were big runs of humpback, dog salmon, and occasionally even sockeye.

In his oral history recorded for the Elphinstone Pioneer Museum, Robert MacKay tells of building a fishing boat out of shakes in 1937 when he was fourteen, and of obtaining a commercial fishing license two years later. "I fished at the head of Bargain Harbour, just out from the bridge there, and I caught a thousand fish that summer. You see, the big salmon they weren't worth nothing. If you could sell them you'd get two cents a pound for them, and usually you couldn't sell them at all. So we usually threw them overboard. Took up too much room in a little boat, you know."

By 1950 dwindling salmon stocks prompted the government to close Jervis Inlet to net fishing. Slowly other conservation regulations began to appear, but most were too late. In addition to over-fishing, streams producing fish had also been mismanaged. Logging companies, such as those operating at Vancouver River, didn't like the smell of rotting salmon that died in nearby streams after they spawned. Their solution was to bulldoze or dike the spawning channels so the salmon could no longer use them. For nearly a hundred years industrial and household wastes were poured untreated into streams and inlets, while toxic chemicals seeped into the ocean from pulp mills at Woodfibre and Port Mellon and were joined by acid from the slag piles at the Britannia copper mine.

The late 1990s saw a change in attitude on the Sunshine Coast as local First Nations people, Interfor, environmentalists, commercial and recreational fishermen, and government agencies began working together to turn this environmental tragedy into a productive fishery by rebuilding dwindling fish stocks, rehabilitating damaged streams, and making sure stricter anti-pollution laws were enforced.

At hatcheries salmon are being raised for stock development. "Our creeks have been so badly damaged," says hatchery volunteer John Alvarez, "that

there is not enough water, protection, or nourishment for the fry to survive the time they need to be in fresh water. Depending on the species, this time can be from two to sixteen months. The hatcheries give them a safe pool with all the water and food they need to mature to smolts."

Sechelt Inlet's McLean Bay Hatchery, constructed in 1979, is owned and operated by the Sechelt Indian Band, with funding assistance from the federal fisheries department. Returning chinook, coho, chum, and pink brood stock are seined and trapped in Mclean Bay in the fall. Eggs from the pinks and chums are incubated at the hatchery and grown out in net pens. When they are over two grams and have "buttoned up," which means their egg sac has been absorbed and they begin to look like

A young angler looks curiously at the fish she has just caught in the Chapman Creek Hatchery trout pond. Trout especially raised for sale help fund the hatchery's salmon enhancement efforts.

The Chapman Creek Hatchery

In 1985 amid the Sunshine Coast's salmon farming boom the million-dollar Chapman Creek Hatchery was built by Cockburn Bay Seafarms, owned by Tom and Linda May. After changing owners twice, it was finally purchased in 1992 by the Sunshine Coast Salmonid Enhancement Society for $150,000 with funds raised within the local community and the greater Vancouver area. Each year approximately one million salmon are nurtured here for anywhere from two to sixteen months, and then released into Roberts Creek, Chaster Creek, Anderson Creek, and Sakinaw Lake for stock development. They are also released into the local terminal fishery areas: Halfmoon Bay, Porpoise Bay, Davis Bay, and Chapman Creek, which is the only creek on the Sunshine Coast where you can fish and retain coho and chinook salmon.

Funded through public donations, government grants, and the sale of live hatchery-grown trout, the facility is designed for public use. It contains living quarters with office and workroom space below, and an incubation unit with a capacity for three million eggs—although only half of that is currently being used—and 34 grow-out tanks that are all in use at different times. Classroom and conference room rentals are available in the William G. Chinnick educational building where students from kindergarten to grade twelve learn about all aspects of salmon and salmonid enhancement. On the banks of Chapman Creek are picnic areas, horseshoe pits, and a viewing platform where visitors can watch salmon spawning. Children are encouraged to come and catch their own trout—with the help of a hatchery guide—from one of the tanks, and an annual open house event is held each summer with a special package price that usually includes a hot dog and cold drink, face painting, and catching two trout to take home.

Since 1993 the hatchery has been managed by Bob Anstead who came to the Sunshine Coast in 1986 to build an aquaculture hatchery for Aquarius Seafarms at Gray Creek. With a 30-year background in raising salmon, trout, and steelhead in California, Oregon, and British Columbia, Bob can't say enough about the economic benefits of salmon enhancement to the community. "We've been getting memberships from people coming to look at the creek. They're staying on the coast a week at a time just for the coho that are coming back."

The Chapman Creek Hatchery is open to the public. Guided tours of the Sechelt Indian Band Salmon Hatchery at Maclean Bay can be arranged by calling 604-885-5562.

salmon, they are released into the bay—usually around the same time as naturally incubated salmon from the creeks are entering Sechelt and Jervis inlets and Hotham Sound. Coho eggs are sent to the Chapman Creek hatchery where they are incubated and kept until they are smolts and can survive in the salt water, at which time they are released back into McLean Bay. The chinook caught are used as a food fish.

Under contract with the Department of Fisheries and Oceans, every year the hatchery receives approximately 150,000 smolts transplanted from Lang Creek, and 150,000 coho smolts transplanted from Capilano River stock. For two and a half weeks they are kept at McLean Bay and "imprinted" with Shannon Creek water, which is pumped into their net pens. The imprint programs them to return to Shannon Creek rather than to their birth waters.

The goal of the McLean Bay hatchery, says manager Darlene Nooski, is "to get to the point where we're no longer needed; where the returns will be so good the fish don't need us anymore."

Local salmon enhancement also includes working with other citizen groups, government agencies, and industry. Each year, for example, the Powell River Salmon Society donates 150,000 chinook eggs to the Sunshine Coast Salmon Enhancement Society. The eggs are incubated at a hatchery that Howe Sound Pulp and Paper Ltd. have built at their Port Mellon mill. Heated wastewater from the mill enables the eggs to be incubated at ten degrees Celsius all winter. When they've reached two grams, the fry are transferred to a hatchery at Soames Creek, built by the late William G. Chinnick. By March the now three-gram fingerlings are moved to the Chapman Creek hatchery and nurtured until May when they are released into Chapman Creek.

Although much is being done to heal the fishery, with the exception of prawn, black cod, and crab, no local commercial catches have been allowed in recent years. Where once up to five hundred fish boats operated out of Gibsons and Pender Harbour, there are now less than two hundred.

Craig Perry and his wife Tamara dealt with the declining stocks by turning from fishing to operating the Beldis Fish Company at the Gibsons Wharf. Purchasing direct from commercial fish boats that come into the harbour, they sell flash-frozen lingcod, black cod, quill-back rock cod, and troll-caught salmon, as well as locally caught shrimp, prawns, and crab. Also sold are a few items from a processing plant, such as sole and lingcod fillets, cold-smoked lox, hot-smoked salmon, and salmon jerky from farmed salmon.

Aquaculture began on the Sunshine Coast on June 6, 1972, when Allan C. Meneely obtained the first aquaculture licence ever issued in British Columbia by the federal Department of Fisheries and Oceans for the Moccasin

Billy Griffith

For seiners like Egmont's William "Billy" Griffith, who has been fishing for the past 52 years, closures to the Sunshine Coast commercial fishery have meant that all of his fishing must be done in the north. "I only have one licence," he explains. "To fish the whole coast you need three licences. I can't afford three."

Billy agrees with the closures for seine fishermen. He also believes that because of Department of Fisheries and Oceans (DFO) field staff shortages the fishery is not being monitored efficiently. "Our fishery is bent, not broken," he says. "If DFO would resume management, we'd be in difficulties, not in trouble."

As Chairman of the Pender Harbour Wildlife Society's Salmon Committee, Billy has spent the past twenty years working on salmon enhancement projects, including helping to build and run the Lions Park Hatchery.

Valley Marifarms, located close to Earls Cove on Agamemnon Channel. The industry peaked in 1988 with 48 salmon farms, four processing plants, and at least seven private hatcheries on the Sunshine Coast. By 1992 only four farms remained, and all of them belonged to Target Marine Products Ltd. This locally-owned company also runs the Egmont Fish Plant Ltd., which began operation in 1987, and the Gray Creek Hatchery on Sechelt Inlet, once a part of Aquarius Sea Farms' holdings. Here, besides developing fish stocks for their farms, Target is working with the Malaspina University College to study Fraser River white sturgeon born in captivity. A building containing three large tanks and four small ones was constructed for the study, which they hope will determine the viability of farming sturgeon commercially for meat and caviar production.

Roger Engeset's company, Wood Bay Salmon Farms, was once one of the major players in the aquaculture boom with a farm and processing plant at Wood Bay. When algal blooms forced him to close the farm in 1990, Roger sold the site and moved his processing equipment to a new location on Field Road. Today Wood Bay Seafoods Ltd. continues to process salmon for markets in eastern Canada, Japan, and Mexico. Their products include salmon that is hot smoked, cold smoked, and marinated, as well as salmon jerky and fashimi. Throughout the year the plant hires from twenty to a hundred employees, depending on the orders they receive and how fast they must be processed.

Shellfish have been farmed successfully on the Sunshine Coast since 1923 when Ian McKechnie's father secured an oyster lease for his son at Oyster Bay

A storm approaches Bay Fresh Seafoods Ltd.,
Vancouver Bay, Jervis Inlet in November 1985.

in Pender Harbour. Although McKechnie had little interest in tending oyster beds, his oysters spawned local populations that continued to grow and today provide a limited wild fishery. McKechnie hired his neighbour, Bill Klein, to look after the beds and paid him with oyster seed, which Klein used to establish his own beds across the bay.

With Dr. Dan Quayle's introduction in the 1950s of off-bottom culture—suspending oysters from rafts or floats—oyster culture spread from a few areas with suitable beaches to the deeper waters of Sechelt and Jervis Inlets. Today there are ten companies farming oysters locally. One of these is Pearl Seaproducts Inc., founded in 1986 by Sam Bowman, Drew Standfield, Stuart Evans, and Rick Reynolds. They have two farm sites in Jervis Inlet and two in Sechelt Inlet, a processing plant in Garden Bay, and 40 employees. With an inventory of twenty million oysters the company ships to markets in the United States and Asia. Pearl Seaproducts is the first oyster producer in Canada to export live oysters to Japan. Their flash-frozen oysters in the shell won the grand prize for excellence in value-added seafood marketing at the 2000 B.C. Seafood Sensations competition.

Rock Extraction-Related Work

Since before the turn of the last century granite, gravel, marble, dolomite, wollastonite, garnet, and even a small amount of gold and copper have been mined on the Sunshine Coast. Granite was quarried on Nelson Island as early

*Children play in the sand while a man-sized sandpile is
created behind them at Construction Aggregate Ltd.'s Open House.*

as 1894, and on Norwest Bay Road in 1912. Gravel was mined from local
beaches by George Glassford and George Soames in Gibsons, and by Herbert
Whitaker in Sechelt.

For more than 50 years Champion and White operated gravel pits at
Howe Sound. Their company was purchased by Ocean Construction Supplies
(OCS), whose subsidiary Hillside Sand & Gravel began excavating near Port
Mellon in 1942. This operation was taken over by another OCS subsidiary,
Construction Aggregates Ltd., in 1974. Before it closed, the pit provided more
than 750,000 tonnes of granular fill to reclaim the 159-acre Expo 86 site.

Today Construction Aggregates Ltd.'s open pit sand and gravel mine
overlooking the town of Sechelt is one of the largest in North America,
producing approximately five million tons of aggregates each year. It opened
in 1989 when the company was given a lease on crown land in exchange for
the Hillside Sand & Gravel site. The processing plant is built on land leased
from the Sechelt Indian Band. Their products, which include fill materials,
road bases, golf course sand, crushed rock, and washed aggregates, are carried
by conveyor belt from the plant to a loading facility in Trail Bay where they
are transferred to barges and hauled to markets in Vancouver and California.

Now owned by Lehigh Portland Cement (North America), a subsidiary
of Heidelberger Zement in Germany, Construction Aggregates Ltd. employs
63 people. A recently expanded loading facility in Trail Bay is expected to
increase that number by another fifteen to eighteen full-time positions. Each

Geology at a Glance

Like the rest of the Georgia Lowland, the geologic history of the Sunshine Coast began when igneous rocks were raised into mountain ranges, eroded by glaciers, raised again, and eroded once more. About 250 million years ago the eroded segments subsided to below or at sea level, where they remained for the next 100 million years. While dinosaurs evolved, declined, and then vanished from the earth, layer after layer of marine sediment settled over the igneous rock.

The Cretaceous Period, which began 130 million years ago, was marked by earthquakes and volcanoes that faulted and folded the land lying under the sea, thrusting it upward until it formed the tops of the Coast Range mountains that were gradually covered with marine sediment. Now molten granite pushed upward from deep within the earth, cooled, and crystalized before it broke through the softer igneous and sedimentary layers.

As the earthquakes and volcanoes continued, the granite separated and the cracks, sometimes half a mile wide, were filled with molten rock. Further earthquakes closed the cracks, compacting the new rock within the granite. The climate grew warmer and wetter causing subtropical plants to grow. Rivers flowed and wore away the softer sedimentary and igneous rocks, their routes shifting whenever they encountered the hard granite bedrock.

When the Pleistocene Ice Age arrived one million years ago, glaciers crept across the land. Rock and house-sized boulders became frozen to the undersides of the glaciers and acted like giant rasps. As these ice fields subsided the sea level rose to roughly six hundred feet higher than it is today and the Sechelt Peninsula became an island.

Between ten thousand and twelve thousand years ago the sea subsided and the shoreline remained close to its present level. By then the land was covered with glacial till (clay or sand) in alternating layers with marine and river sediments, and capped with cobbles and boulders.

September the company holds an open house, inviting the public to a free barbecue and bus tour of the mine site—including a stop at one of the best views on the Sunshine Coast. Among the features pointed out is the company's reclamation project which uses bio-solids from waste treatment plants to fertilize grasses, shrubs, and trees planted in soils left behind from the mining. Poplar trees sown several years ago now provide shade for grand fir seedlings planted in the spring of 2001.

While many people grumble that the quarry is a noisy, dusty eyesore, others are fascinated by its sculptured plateaus and ridges that offer a glimpse at the mysteries lying deep beneath the surface. Although the company does not pay local taxes, they do donate $103,000 annually to community projects, helping to fund everything from sports activities to school breakfast programs, music festivals, arts programs, and the Festival of the Written Arts. Construction Aggregates Ltd. also provided most of the funding for the new Sechelt walking pier.

Other gravel operations that continue to operate successfully on the Sunshine Coast include Jack Sewe Ltd's quarry at Treat or Beaver Creek, which was started in 1966, and the Lafarge Concrete gravel operation on the east side of Sechelt Inlet, just north of the Skookumchuck Rapids.

The Sechelt Steamship Company

To ensure regular service for his Sechelt Hotel and logging camps, Herbert Whitaker launched the Sechelt Steamship Company in 1903. His first ship was a 52.5-foot converted steam tug called the *New Era,* which was eventually used for logging and passenger trade on Sechelt, Salmon, and Narrows Inlets. The 73-foot coal-burning screw steamer, *Hattie Hansen,* which Herbert renamed the *Sechelt,* and a former steam tug from Scotland called the *Tartar* operated from Ward's Wharf at the foot of Abbott Street in Vancouver, ending their runs at Donley's Wharf in Pender Harbour. The 172-ton wooden-hulled *Belcarra* was purchased in 1910 and used to serve the logging camps of Jervis Inlet.

Built as lake steamers, Whitaker's ships were too long, narrow, and high to provide the stability required to navigate safely along the Pacific coast. After being wrecked near Canoe Reef in 1909, the *New Era* was sold. The *Belcarra* went aground in 1910 and sank in Agamemnon Channel. Although crew and passengers were saved, the loss of these ships and strengthening competition from other day-steamer lines induced Whitaker to liquidate his shipping business. The *Sechelt* was sold in January 1911 to the British Columbia Steamship Company. Two months later she was caught in a storm between Victoria and Sooke and went down with all hands. The *Tartar* was eventually sold to Sir John Jackson and Company, who converted her back into a tug, and then again in 1927 to the Hopkins brothers who brought her back to the Sunshine Coast as the *Hawser.* In 1937 she was sold for scrap.

The first wharf on Porpoise Bay was built by Bert Whitaker in 1902. The first government wharf was construction in 1923 close to Whitaker's, but extended out into the bay rather than running parallel to the bluff.

3

A Place Where Wharves Still Exist

If they were not pounded apart by waves and driftwood during winter storms, the early wooden wharves of the Sunshine Coast were eventually eaten by teredos and rot. But no matter how great or frequent their destruction, they were always rebuilt because they were such a vital part of each settlement. They were a gathering place where business was conducted and news was shared while waiting for the steamboat to arrive with mail and to discharge or take on passengers and cargo. They were also the gateways to seaside resorts that brought thousands of tourists to the coast each summer.

The vitality of local wharves lasted until Black Ball Ferries began operating a run between Horseshoe Bay and Gibsons Landing in 1951, and between Earls Cove and Saltery Bay in 1952. Their docks, like the present BC Ferries terminals at Langdale and Earls Cove, were designed for speed and efficiency of loading. Today instead of gathering on the dock, most passengers stay in their cars. There are no bands playing, no friends or neighbours to talk with, and no community leaders waiting—as hotel owner Bert Whitaker once did— to greet new arrivals with a cheerful, "It's been a long winter, hasn't it? But now that you are here, the sun is shining!"

In *Whistle Up the Inlet* Gerald A. Rushton tells of 250 passengers enjoying an excursion trip in 1891 to Irvines Landing where Charles Irvine had a hotel and post office. When Joe Gonsalves purchased the property in 1904, he and Theodore Dames built a new hotel, saloon, and store at the head of the wharf. A few concrete remnants of those buildings still remain near the beach, and there is a small pub, open during the spring and summer, on the site of their old café.

Ownership of the public wharf at Irvines Landing was transferred to the Department of Fisheries and Oceans (DFO) by a 1982 federal Order in Council, which also included the public wharves at Egmont, Madeira Park, Whiskey Slough, Secret Cove, Porpoise Bay, Davis Bay, Gibsons, and West Bay. With a mandate to maintain these wharves for use by the commercial fishing

Waiting for the steamboat at Sechelt wharf, 1916.

Waiting for the steamboat at Roberts Creek, 1935.
SS Lady Cecilia *coming into the wharf.*

industry, the DFO in turn developed local Harbour Authorities, each with their own elected board of directors. "The Harbour Authority is responsible for day-to-day activities," says Levi Timmerans, from DFO's Small Craft Harbour's Branch. "We are responsible for capital projects. In this way the money stays in communities, and local users have a say in what happens on their wharf."

In 1999 the Harbour Authority of Pender Harbour initiated a major waterfront revitalization project at Madeira Park through the Pender Harbour Authority Foundation. With funding from the provincial and federal governments, and local donations ranging from two to ten thousand dollars, the Foundation constructed a retaining wall and back-filled it, thus reclaiming a portion of the waterfront. An office building, park, and picnic area were built on the new site and the wharf facilities were upgraded, with better power outlets for boats, a marine sewage pump-out system, showers, and washrooms. Seaplane floats from Billings Bay were installed at Whiskey Slough to be mainly used by fishermen. One float has a secure shed where nets can be repaired.

Guests to Herbert Whitaker's hotel, opened in 1899, were initially ferried to and from the steamships by rowboat. By 1902 he had built a wharf at Porpoise Bay to handle marine traffic from the loggers and miners working in camps along Sechelt, Salmon, and Narrows Inlets. Two years later he constructed a wharf that extended from his store out into Trail Bay.

When the Union Steamship Company bought the bankrupt Whitaker estate in 1926 the excursion trade was at its peak. Chain stores such as Woodward's and the Hudson's Bay Company held their annual staff picnics at Sechelt and the wharf was crowded with day tourists disembarking on a Saturday or Sunday morning. They would stroll along the boulevard, stop at the General Store or tearoom, play a game of tennis on the courts behind the dance pavilion, or join in the festivities at the picnic grounds, which extended from what is now the corner of Wharf and Cowrie to the Royal Canadian Legion. In the evening they would catch the boat back to Vancouver. Former Sechelt postal clerk W. J. "Jack" Mayne could remember stamping almost a thousand postcards in one day, and seeing three Union steamships at the wharf on a Sunday–the *Lady Alexandra, Lady Cecelia,* and *Lady Cynthia.*

The federal government purchased the Trail Bay wharf and kept it operational until regular ferry service eliminated the need for a steamboat stop at Sechelt. The wharf was torn down after it was severely damaged by fire in 1970.

In 2000, Construction Aggregates Ltd., who were enlarging their loading facility in Trail Bay, funded most of the construction costs for a new Sechelt pier that was built near the site of the original government wharf. The Sechelt Downtown Business Association (SDBA)—whose future plans include floats

*Roberts Creek wharf in 1926 with Bailey's Store at the end
and Harry Robert's "castle" on the shore to the right.*

where cruise ships can dock and a park to be located on the site of Whitaker's second hotel—initiated the project. "We see it as a focal point for families, community groups, and tourists," says Deb Hodgkin of the SDBA.

Early Roberts Creek settlers had to row to a government float anchored a thousand feet offshore to connect with the steamships, and it wasn't until 1914 that a government dock was finally constructed. An approach to the new landing was funded and built by local volunteers, organized by Harry Roberts. As in other areas, the pier soon became a gathering place for the community. In *Remembering Roberts Creek*, Mary Covernton O'Brien writes: "As teenagers, we also used the wharf for our evening escapades … it was great fun to occasionally haul out our portable wind-up gramophone and proceed to have a moonlit dance. Many a youthful romance was started at the end of the old wharf!"

Although it was rebuilt and repaired many times, the dock gradually disintegrated and was finally torn down in 1970. The breakwater that remained was used as a propane storage facility. In 1987 property beside the mouth of Roberts Creek was purchased and designated as a park by the Sunshine Coast Regional District (SCRD). The propane tanks were removed and a walkway was built along the breakwater ending in a platform reminiscent of an old-style wharf. On summer evenings fire spinners use this area to practise and the light from their flaming batons shimmers on the water below. Throughout the year community events are held here, including Earth Day celebrations

Boats moored at the Gibsons public wharf, maintained by the Department of Fisheries and Oceans through the Gibsons Landing Harbour Authority.

and the Creek Daze festival, where people dance to music broadcast over electronic speakers.

The first dock in Gibsons was built with a homemade pile driver and windlass by George Gibson Sr. and his two sons about two hundred feet south of the present government wharf. From his house located just above and slightly west of the present Molly's Reach Restaurant, George could see arriving boats. Often it was after midnight when a ship's whistle would rouse him from his bed, and with lantern in hand, he would hurry to the dock to collect and send off mailbags and other freight.

Although it has been rebuilt many times, the Gibsons government wharf dates back to 1901. It is owned by the DFO, and managed by the Gibsons Landing Harbour Authority. In 1999 they joined with the Gibsons Economic Development partnership, the town, and the Chamber of Commerce to upgrade the facility. Besides the addition of new floats and installation of a sewage pump-out station, they built a wharfinger's office, which contains a meeting room, washrooms, showers, and laundry facilities. A promenade and gazebo were constructed on top of the adjoining breakwater, providing a picturesque walk and an excellent viewing spot for events such as the outrigger canoe races, sailing regattas, and Sea Cavalcade logger sports. "That dock is

View of the wharves from the shore of Irvines Landing.

trippers who take the *Dogwood Princess* ferry to Keats Landing so they can hike to Plumper Cove Marine Park. Gambier's Port Graves dock is also used by hikers and for search and rescue teams.

In 2000, when Transport Canada decided to divest itself of eight local docks, a referendum was held to determine whether the SCRD should take them over. Whereas Pender Harbour, Sechelt, and the Sechelt Indian Band opted out of the decision—their docks being owned and funded by the DFO—56 percent of those who did cast their ballot were in favour of the takeover. The SCRD, however, has the option of closing any of the wharves that prove to be too expensive for them to maintain.

Although their future is uncertain, the wharves on the Sunshine Coast still play an important part in the lives of the people who make this part of the world their home, or who come here for a holiday. They began as community efforts and they seem destined to continue as community efforts. All that's missing is a courtly gentleman doffing his straw hat and saying, "It's been a long winter, hasn't it?"

4

4

ℐ Place Where People Communicate

Before European settlement the Sechelt First Nation communicated with other tribes through messengers who would memorize detailed orations from their chief, and relay them to tribes up and down the coast, and into the interior regions of the province.

Having no messengers in their culture, pioneer families would go to great lengths to establish and maintain a postal service, which was their only means of communicating with the world beyond the Sunshine Coast. On his trips to Vancouver in the *Swamp Angel*, George Gibson would collect mail for Howe Sound residents from the main post office in Vancouver. In 1892 he became the official postmaster and built a small post office in a shack behind his house. When he resigned nine years later, no immediate replacement could be found so he simply collected outgoing mail, which he handed to the ship's purser, and left incoming mail in a wooden box fastened to the freight shed. Residents would sort through the pile, pick out their own mail, and return the rest to the box.

In 1904, Frank Roberts would row an aboriginal dugout canoe into the bay on mail days to meet the Union Steamship *Comox* and collect any letters destined for Roberts Creek.

For a while after an altercation with Herbert Whitaker, who became postmaster of Sechelt in 1896, the Union Steamships refused to call in at the Sechelt Wharf. Consequently, Norm Burley would haul the mail to Selma Park in the community bus, which was little more than a truck with wooden benches. Knowing how delighted the steamship captain would be to sail without Whitaker's mail, Norm often drove at breakneck speeds over the rough road, ignoring his passengers' frantic attempts to bribe him into slowing down.

Walter Wray was managing a post office and store for Leonard Bailey in 1917 when it was sold to a Japanese-Canadian, George Hatashita. After convincing the government that no "alien Japanese" could hold public office,

Egmont Post Office and community notice board.

Wray put the post office onto a float and towed it to his own place. Ten years later it was restored to Hatashita, who by then had been joined by his daughter Kay and son-in-law Ted Hyashi.

Newspapers on the Sunshine Coast have played a major role not only as communicators of important information and events, but also as a record of the people and changes that have affected its communities in the past 70 years. Many publications have been short-lived, but they have all stayed long enough to be missed.

The first paper, started in 1930, was a weekly two-page, foolscap newsletter mimeographed by the Reverend C.O. Darby. It ended a year later when Darby was dismissed after an altercation with his church. His newsletter was followed in 1939 by a six-page, coast-wide newspaper that Kathleen and Terence O'Neil of Roberts Creek published; they were bankrupt within three months. Other papers such as the *Peninsula Independent, Peninsula Times,* the *Peninsula Voice,* the *Leader,* and *The Press* lasted longer, but eventually closed because they were unable to survive on the limited advertising dollars available on the coast.

Although it changed owners several times, the *Coast News* was the longest running newspaper. Started in Halfmoon Bay in 1945 by Ernie Parr Pearson of Sechelt and Al Alsgaard of Powell River, it was moved to Gibsons four years later. After a successful 50-year run, latterly by The Glassford Press Ltd., the newspaper was sold to an Alberta-based chain, which closed it down in January 1995 when the newly unionized staff attempted to negotiate their first contract.

Suddenly finding themselves without a newspaper to write for, *Coast News* employees Jane Seyd, Darah Hansen, Sue Connor, Andy Jukes, and Joel Johnstone formed their own company, the SunCoast News Group, Inc., and on February 13, 1995 began publishing the *Coast Independent*. During its six years of operation this paper won national and provincial awards, including the 2001 B.C. and Yukon Community Newspapers Association selection as one of the top three papers for "General Excellence" in its circulation class. In March 2001 the *Coast Independent* was sold to Vancouver-based Madison Publishing Ltd.

A second newspaper, established in April 1997 as *The Sunshine Coast Reporter,* is owned by publisher Peter Kvarnstrom and the Madison Publishing Company. It was a finalist for both the 2001 British Columbia Arts Council Arts and Cultural Award and the Neville Shanks Memorial Award for historical writing. Merged with the *Coast Independent* in March 2001 and renamed the *Coast Reporter,* the paper has a circulation of 13,000 and covers local news from Port Mellon to Egmont.

In 1990 Myrtle Winchester, a former editor of the *Coast News,* started the *Harbour Spiel.* "I phoned the late Al Lloyd, a wonderful Pender Harbour historian, and asked him to write a piece about Christmas in Pender Harbour fifty years ago," she said. "Got a few other things in there and approached some businesses. After it came out, people kept asking if I'd put out another one." Today Myrtle's paper is published monthly and brings Pender Harbour News to more than 1,500 readers.

Communication on the Sunshine Coast achieved a new dimension when Northwest Communications Ltd., a company owned by Stan Thomas, introduced cablevision in September 1970. In 1982 Stan's children purchased the Sunshine Coast operations from Northwest Communications Ltd. and formed Coast Cable Vision Ltd. that later became Coast Cable Communications Ltd.

In 2001 Coast Cable received the B.C. Principals' and Vice-Principals' Association Partnership Award to commemorate a partnership between the cable company and School District No. 46. Their unique relationship began in 1978 when the Thomas family was approached by Maryanne West and Elphinstone teacher Marta MacKown to give wider exposure to video documentaries being prepared by Elphinstone Student Research Productions, developed by Marta and her social studies students. As a result, School District No. 46, the cable company, and Marta established a six-course program to be taken over a two-year period, which enables students to earn credits towards graduation. The primary role of the channel, says John Thomas, is public affairs programming. "But," he adds, "they don't stop there! The students of Marta's career prep program are the station's primary volunteers and they are in the field covering all sorts of community events and issues." The numbers of students who have gone on to full-time careers in the film or broadcast industry further reflects the success of

Telephones on the Sunshine Coast

Telephone service to the Sunshine Coast began in 1910 when a telephone line was strung from Egmont to Seaside Park and to the Port Mellon paper mill. Telephones were located at Whitaker's General Store in Sechelt, and at the homes of Dr. Frederick Inglis and and Lou and Harry Winn who managed the telephone service in Gibsons. In 1913, service was extended between Sechelt and Vancouver, and by 1946 the Winns' exchange had become so busy that Harry had to move it from his home to an office he built next door. This tiny building, halfway up the hill from lower Gibsons, is now Jack 's Lane Bistro and Bakery.

The B.C. Telephone Company purchased the exchange from the Winns in 1953 and immediately implemented 24-hour service. Today Sunshine

Coast residents have almost the same service as Vancouver. Cell phones also operate effectively on the coast, although there are a few "dead" spots.

Lou and Harry Winn outside the door of the Gibsons telephone exchange.

the program. "It's hard to tell an exact number," says Marta MacKown, "because we don't keep in touch with all of them. But there have been at least 24. One student who graduated from the program ten years ago just enrolled at BCIT[3] to obtain further training in broadcasting."

Coast Cable also provides all three Sunshine Coast secondary schools with annual scholarships, and a district-wide scholarship to honour Marta MacKown and Maryanne West. In addition they provide jobs for twenty employees and support numerous initiatives and groups on the Coast. Technically they offer a broad selection of analog services and dozens of digital services. Most signals are received via multiple satellites, but a few travel via microwave at their Davis Bay site. They are also the primary provider of high-speed Internet access on the Coast.

The other major Internet service provider on the coast was started in 1994 when Scott and Luinda Bleackley founded Sunshine Net Inc. They had 2,200 subscribers in February 1999 when they sold the business to Uniserve Online.

In 1997 Sechelt resident Laurie McConnell developed the main Sunshine Coast web page, Big Pacific.com. Continually expanding, the site has over five hundred pages with audio and real video, slide shows, listings for tourism and commercial businesses, text and photo albums on arts, culture, history, and wildlife.

While Jill Baxter helped research the business section, Heather Till provided historical data. "I always keep in mind that I am only one voice in a community of thirty thousand people," says Laurie. "I try to include other writers, and I have a staff that helps." Big Pacific.com now has six full-time employees, as well as up to five subcontractors and six sales staff members. "Many people who come here never heard of the Sunshine Coast until they read about it on the web site," she says. "Conservatively, the value it brings to the local economy is half a million dollars."

Although the Sunshine Coast seems well supplied with communication services, should a disaster wipe them all out, the Sunshine Coast Amateur Radio Club is prepared to provide emergency radio communication. Each of the club's members has a licence and a ham radio and has trained with the SCRD's Emergency Preparedness team. At the end of each June club members join in a field day sponsored by the Amateur Radio Relay League in the U.S., setting up a field station with minimal resources. In 1999 one inventive operator used a bow and arrow to transport his antenna to a treetop. "We do it for fun, and it also provides at least one day where everyone can get out and practise emergency techniques," says club president, Dorian Gregory.

5

A Place of Music

On the packed-earth centre floor of the Sechelt Longhouse a young boy, wearing a long-beaked wooden mask and a woven blanket patterned with blue and white Thunderbird motifs, dances and sings to the beat of a deerskin drum. Students from the local elementary school watch from the bleachers encircling the stage, enthralled.

The boy is telling a story following the customs of his ancestors who used songs and dances to pass along tribal history, celebrate special events, and in healing ceremonies conducted by shamans. When such rituals were outlawed in the late 1800s, the musical talents of the Sechelt native people were channelled into church choirs and large uniformed brass bands, and it wasn't until the 1970s that they once again felt safe enough to publicly display their traditional music.

Florence Dubois in her family history, "William Jeffries and Other Pioneers of the Sunshine Coast," tells of dances at the Indian Band Hall during the 1930s. "They had a complete brass band and there was one man in particular … who could play every instrument in the band, which consisted of about seven pieces. His name was Reggie Paul."

For the Coast's pioneer settlers, music was a way to escape the hardships of wrestling a living from an untamed land. According to Francis Wyngaert in *The West Howe Sound Story*, when the Finnish settlers in Gibsons built the Socialist Hall in 1910, "its initial purpose [was] as a dance hall." Four years later Bert Whitaker was holding Saturday night dances at his second Sechelt Hotel. Musicians were brought in from off the coast, or garnered from the local citizenry.

As the population of the Sunshine Coast increased, so did its supply of musically talented people. In the 1980s former Elphinstone Secondary graduate and international opera and concert singer Lyn Vernon returned to Gibsons and started teaching singing. She formed a choir and an orchestra and eventually

Community Dances

Pioneer schools in even the smallest Sunshine Coast communities were transformed into concert halls at Christmas and Easter, and into dance halls on Saturday nights.

In their oral histories at the Elphinstone Pioneer Museum, Cledia Duncan (née Warnock) and Wilfred "Tiffy" Wray recall dances at the Maple Leaf School in Donley's Landing, when Doris Dusenbury would play the piano and her husband Roy the accordion. In later years, according to Cledia, they "used to hire the Indian band to come up from Sechelt and play for the dances." At the Irvines Landing Hall the Macleod family played the piano, drums, accordion, and violin.

When he was not running his trucking business Eric Inglis, son of Dr. Fred Inglis, played saxophone and clarinet in the Howe Sounders orchestra, which was organized in the early 1930s. "In those days, to go to Sechelt was an event," recalls his widow, Lenore Inglis. "Eric went because he played at the dances and he always had the truck." In the 1940s his brother Hugh was part of the Roberts Creek String Orchestra.

Lenore's cousin Pearle Tretheway (née Chamberlin) remembers dances at the pavilions in Sechelt and Selma Park: "Orchestras used to come up from Vancouver. We always went to those. We travelled in the rumble seat of somebody's old car and ate all the dust. It was fun."

The Sechelt Indian Brass Band at the opening
of Our Lady of the Rosary Church in 1890.

Sunshine Coast Introductory Orchestra, May 1995.

the Sunshine Coast Music Society through which she put on musicals such as *Jesus Christ Superstar* and *Anne of Green Gables*. When she resigned after ten years, the Music Society went on to produce *Pirates of Penzance* and *HMS Pinafore*, among others. Now more than twelve choirs belong to the society, offering music that ranges from the eclectic repertoire of the Soundwaves Choir to the barbershop harmony of Arbutus Sounds and the throaty Balkan music of Sokole. Lyn Vernon is currently producing musical events for local venues including The Club in Gibsons.

Violin teacher Michelle Bruce got together with conductor Tom Kershaw in 1992 and started the Sunshine Coast Community Orchestra, which in less than ten years has grown to six levels, from the Introductory Orchestra conducted by Michelle, to the Community Symphony Orchestra conducted by David Suomi-Marttinen.

Equally zealous, but determined to present classical works exactly as they were written, Tom Kershaw left the Community Orchestra in 1995 to develop the Sunshine Coast Philharmonic Orchestra.

After the B.C. Ferry Corporation cancelled regular late night sailings in 1982 many coast residents found it was too costly to stay overnight to attend Vancouver concerts. That's when Alan Crane, a local teacher and music lover, started a series of subscription concerts, bringing first-class performers to the

Sunshine Coast Community Introductory Orchestra, 1998.

coast. In 1992 he formed The Coast Recital Society, which presents concerts every winter at the Raven's Cry Theatre with groups such as The Schubert Ensemble of London, and Angela Cheng & The Diaz Trio. On alternate weekends, the Pender Harbour Music Society presents performances at the Pender Harbour School of Music, their schedule including Duo Constanzi and Robert Silverman. The Live Music Society of Roberts Creek is bringing other popular entertainers to the coast such as "gypsy" musicians, Willie and Lobo.

Each spring for the past 26 years a coast-wide eleven-day Festival of the Performing Arts (formerly the Sunshine Coast Music Festival) has been held, and the talents of more than a thousand local music students adjudicated by a visiting panel of internationally acclaimed musicians.

During the warmer seasons a different kind of music hits the coast. Annual summer jazz festivals in Pender Harbour, Roberts Creek, and Gibsons are attracting world-renowned jazz artists such as the Machado Brothers and the Alan Matheson Sextet. Since 1998 Country Music Festivals have been held in Sechelt featuring, among others, the Rankin Family, Prairie Oyster, and Patricia Conroy. Summer music schools have been established in Egmont and Pender Harbour, and music camps for kids are held each year at Davis Bay Elementary.

Sunshine Coast musicians continue to be in great demand and generally their concerts and dances are sold out long before the events. Their roster

Coast String Fiddlers, Spring 1999.

includes the eighteen-piece Roberts Creek Big Band, Jamie Bowers' Moodsingers, Nicki Webbers' Mellowtones, instrumentalists Michael Lacoste and Christian Prekratic of Pulse, vocalists Valerie and Julie Rutter of Gemini, and jazz groups such as Baroque and Blue, and Grooveyard.

Often the local performers seen on stage at night are the friends and neighbours you meet during the day. Maureen Cochrane is a school principal who plays second violin with the Community Symphony along with Dr. Alan Cairns who plays the English horn. Baroque and Blue's drummer Tim Enns can be found most days at his store, Magic Sound Electronics, and well-known potter Pat Forst is a soprano with the Reflections choir.

If you would like to find out about upcoming musical events in a particular area, contact the Arts Hotline at 604-886-4278.

6

The Sunshine Coast Arts Community

A cluster of white clouds hovers over the inlet, its creamy reflection in the dark green waters touched with pinkish hues. All along the shore–among the tall, stately evergreens, the soft moss-yellow banks, and the granite cliffs–are colours and shapes and textures that would titillate any artist's creativity. Add a wide-eyed doe startled along a trail, a curious racoon exploring a summer deck, or a blue heron carefully picking its way across the mud flats, and you might have the reason why the Sunshine Coast has inspired artists since unrecorded times.

Perhaps the earliest of these artists was the primitive sculptor who carved the "Sechelt Image" that now resides at the tem swiya museum in Sechelt. On the museum walls are photos of pictographs painted by ancestors of the Sechelt First Nation, double-headed serpents and stick-like figures that can still be found on rock faces of Jervis, Sechelt, Salmon, and Narrows Inlets, and Sakinaw Lake in Pender Harbour. Around the room special cabinets contain baskets intricately woven from cedar roots and wild cherry bark by native artisans such as Teresa George, Mary Ellen Paul, and Mary Jane Jackson.

Totem poles that once graced the Shishahl longhouses were destroyed and banned under the Oblate system; but using the legends and memories of the elders as guides native carvers began in 1974 to erect new poles to commemorate events in their community. The most recent project includes five poles, four depicting each original Shishalh territory. The fifth pole, which features each clan's traditional crest, is topped by the double eagle crest of the Sechelt Nation, portraying the amalgamation of all the families.

Non-native artists began appearing on the Sunshine Coast in the late 1800s. A collection of miniatures carved by young Herb Steinbrunner, whose father homesteaded in Roberts Creek in 1891, can be found at the Elphinstone Pioneer Museum along with the photographs taken by Helen McCall. Born at Howe Sound in 1899, Helen spent most of the 1920s and 1930s photographing people, events, and scenery from Langdale to Egmont.

Carvings by Herb Steinbrunner at the Elphinstone Pioneer Museum.

Today more than five hundred artists live on the Coast, and private studios and galleries can be found in almost every village and hamlet—a situation that has produced a rather confusing maze of guilds, co-ops, and councils.

The most enduring group has been the Sunshine Coast Arts Council, a non-profit society started in 1965 "to provide opportunities for the community to participate in cultural activities." In the late 1970s the council embarked on a community building project led by Clarke Steabner and funded through a job-training grant to teach log construction. With donated labour, equipment, and supplies, including timber from their own property, Clarke and the others shaped and assembled the logs and erected the Sechelt Arts Centre, which opened in 1979. Since then it has become a favourite venue for local and off-coast art exhibits, musical events, writer's workshops, and summer art programs for children.

The Pender Harbour Artist's Co-operative turned part of the old Forestry Building at Madeira Park into a gallery. Members can exhibit their work for a small membership fee and a few volunteer hours at the gallery. A second group, known as "Harbour Artists," meets weekly during the winter for painting workshops.

In early 1996, a group of artists set about promoting the Sunshine Coast as a centre of the arts. "We were trying," says weaver Barby Paulus, "to develop

The Sechelt Arts Centre that opened in 1979.

an arts co-operative with all kinds of artists, artisans, dancers, and musicians under one umbrella, the final goal being to open a school of the arts. We realize now that an awful lot of it was pie-in-the-sky, but the energy at the meetings was fabulous."

By December they had incorporated as the Gibsons Arts Society (GAS) and part of the membership began fund-raising by painting street banners for the Town of Gibsons, organizing an Artwalk, producing a Christmas arts event supplement for the *Coast Independent*, and managing the Christmas Festival of Lights program at the Wendys-Tim Horton outlet. At the same time Conchita Harding led other members to establish the Sunshine Coast Artists Co-op, aided by a start-up grant from the Ministry of Culture, Small Business and Tourism. The Co-op's Gibsons Landing Gallery was opened on May 30, 1998, and a satellite gallery was set up a few months later in the annex of the Coast Professional Centre. "Conchita gave a year of her life to get that going," says GAS director Peggy Small. In the rented gallery space co-op members can exhibit their work by paying a small commission and volunteering time to the shop. A "Jury and Hanging Committee" decide the arrangement of displays.

With the Co-op taking care of marketing, GAS members turned their attention to developing art classes. In September 2000 that group officially

*Sunshine Coast Quilters Guild display at the
Fibre Arts Festival held in Gibsons.*

changed its name to the Gibsons School of the Arts (GSA), and runs four programs each summer, that—according to organizers Lenore Conacher and Peggy Small—are getting rave reviews for the high quality instruction and personal service participants receive.

The goal of creating an umbrella organization dedicated to promoting the coast as a centre of the arts was taken over by a new group that established the Coast Cultural Alliance in October 1998. This Alliance operates an Arts Hotline, providing callers with information about arts and cultural events happening on the Sunshine Coast. It also publishes a monthly calendar that is available on the ferries and at local arts and retail outlets. More recently the group developed "ARTesia," a program that uses the old Quay Gallery in Molly's Lane for photo exhibits of local artists at work, art and craft demonstrations, a tea room, and coffee night events.

To find out about Sunshine Coast arts and culture events contact the Arts Hotline at 604-886-4278 or <www.bigpacific.com>.

Spinners and Weavers

The mandate of the Sunshine Coast Spinners and Weavers Guild is to keep alive the ancient arts of spinning, weaving, dyeing, and felting by sharing their craft with the public and teaching people to have an appreciation for hand-made objects. The guild has an extensive library of fibre arts books and videos stored at St. John's church in Davis Bay, and a guild loom is kept at Spinsters Loft in Roberts Creek. Every August guild members display their work in Sechelt's Rockwood Annex at the Festival of the Written Arts and in return, volunteer as bartenders, ticket-takers, and other positions at the festival.

Monthly guild meetings include a teaching program, such as Kumihimo, or Japanese braiding. At a more informal monthly meeting, held at Chaster House in Gibsons, participants can bring their spinning wheel, knitting, or other projects and work together.

For more information about the Spinners and Weavers Guild call the Spinsters Loft at 604-886-1465.

Barby Paulus at the loom; Rosemary Klippenstein at the spinning wheel during the Sunshine Coast Fibre Arts Festival in Gibsons. Behind them is a display of quilts crafted by the Sunshine Coast Quilters Guild.

Governor General Adrienne Clarkson meets with Festival of the Written Arts participants in Sechelt. Festival producer Gail Bull (inset) is aided by a force of more than 200 volunteers.

Lining up for autographs with author Shyam Selvadurai at the Festival of the Wrtten Arts.

7

A Place to Write

It's quiet. It's breathtakingly beautiful. It's full of unique individuals. And it's only a ferry's ride away from a metropolis of millions. No wonder that the Sunshine Coast has become a haven for writers including a best-selling romance novelist, top political writers, humourists, biographers and historians, travel writers, poets, novelists, mystery writers, translators, and scientific writers.

Although they didn't have a written language, the Sechelt First Nation passed their history from one generation to another through legends and stories. Many are privately owned by individual families and can't be shared without permission. Elders Gilbert Joe and Theresa Jeffries often tell their tribal stories in Sunshine Coast schools. One legend was used by Sechelt teacher Donna Joe as the basis for her children's book, *Salmon Boy*, published in 1999.

Bertrand Sinclair, the first established writer known to have made the Sunshine Coast his home, began exploring the local waters in his troller *Hoo Hoo* in 1917. His experiences led him to write his best novel, *Poor Man's Rock*, which was about salmon fishing off Lasqueti Island. A year later he moved to Pender Harbour where he continued to write.

Pender Harbour was also a haven for novelist Elizabeth Smart when she rented an old schoolhouse as a home in 1941. Smart was pregnant at the time with the first of her three children–the progeny of her nineteen-year illicit romance with English poet, George Barker.

Journalist, nature-story writer, novelist, and poet Hubert Evans moved his family to Roberts Creek in 1927. Except for a brief period in the 1940s and early 1950s when they lived in northern British Columbia, the family remained at Roberts Creek. In his spare time Evans built himself a double-ended fifteen-foot rowboat that he used to handline salmon in front of his home near the mouth of Stephens Creek, and off Salmon Rock. When he was awarded an honorary university degree from Simon Fraser University in 1984, university Chancellor Paul Cote, and president Robert Saywell came to Evan's home to make the presentation. Fan and fellow-writer, Margaret Laurence, who was also awarded an honorary degree, accompanied them.

By 1983 there were so many writers on the coast, and so much enthusiasm for writing, that an association was formed called "The SunCoast Writers' Forge." Their goals were to share information about writing contests, classes, and markets, sponsor speakers, and publish an annual anthology. The first edition, *Sparks From The Forge*, was published in the fall, in time for the Christmas market. That summer they had succeeded in staging the first Festival of the Written Arts held in Sechelt at the Arts Centre and the Greene Court Recreation Hall. It was such a resounding success that they decided to make the festival an annual event. As subsequent writing festivals proved more and more popular, the gym at Sechelt Elementary was also rented to house the larger audiences who came to hear writers like W. O. Mitchell, Peter Gzowski, and John Gray.

Just before the fifth festival a division occurred within the Forge between those who wanted to concentrate on helping beginning writers, and those who wanted to reach a broader audience by providing programs for readers and writers of all skill-levels. Consequently, in April 1987 the Festival of the Written Arts was incorporated as a separate society, and a series of writers-in-residence workshops was planned, patterned on an experimental program conducted the previous summer in the old Forestry Building at Madeira Park (now the home of the Pender Harbour Music Society). Since it had been unoccupied for many years, the organizers had a major clean-up job to do before the workshops began. "When we turned on the water, the pipes exploded and the garage floor was flooded," says writer and volunteer Gwen Southin. "When we got that fixed we were down on our hands and knees scrubbing up oil and paint. At the same time the men were chopping down brambles that covered the grounds." For sleeping arrangements the women put down cots and sleeping bags in the attic, while the men bunked in what had been the Chief Forester's office. Although there were eighteen participants and only one shower and toilet, the program was a resounding success as instructors Daniel Wood and Aritha Van Herk fuelled the flames of creativity among their students. Many of those writers have since gone on to become published authors.

As the festival expanded to a three-and-a-half day event, even more space was needed. Thus, in 1989 construction began on an outdoor pavilion on the grounds of the Rockwood Lodge. Festival board member and volunteer, David Foss, who managed the project, was assisted by two employees working on a federal government employment grant, and a host of willing volunteers. Constructed entirely of donated B.C. fir and cedar the 480-seat pavilion was

Bev Shaw of Talewind Books supervises book sales at the Rockwood Annex during the Sunshine Coast Festival of the Written Arts.

completed just 30 minutes before Festival #7 was to begin. The building is surrounded by tall trees and fronted by an acre of rhododendrons, magnolias and evergreens. During the festival hanging baskets of flowers grown by local gardeners brighten walkways and open spaces.

To extend the use of the pavilion beyond the festival, the society began scheduling a series of summer concerts—mostly jazz and light classics. In 1994 both the concerts and writer-in-residence programs were discontinued, but the festival continued to feature popular Canadian writers such as John Ralston Saul, Michael Ondaatje, Robert Bringhurst, and up-and-coming authors such as Karen Irving.

Today the four-day Festival of the Written Arts is one of the most popular summer events on the coast, attracting book-lovers from across Canada and the United States. Included in the events is a juried craft fair organized by the Sunshine Coast Arts Council, held at Hackett Park.

The Sechelt and Gibsons Public Library and the Sunshine Coast Arts Centre frequently bring writers to the coast between festivals, or offer their facilities for book launches by newly published Sunshine Coast authors.

To find out more about writing programs on the Sunshine Coast, contact the Festival of the Written Arts at 604-885-9631, or check out their web site at <www.sunshine.net/rockwood>.

A Place to Film

In 1973 the CBC began filming *The Beachcombers*, introducing Nick, Relic, Molly, Jesse, Constable John, and the town of Gibsons to the world. Townspeople grumbled about traffic delays—those being the days before the bypass eliminated the need to go through lower Gibsons—and boaters who tied up at the wharf sometimes had to be bribed with beer to maintain silence while a dock segment was being filmed. For the most part, however, the series had a positive effect on the community, boosting the local economy and providing employment and a lot of fun for those who were hired as extras and background support.

Harry Smith, owner of Smitty's Marina, leased most of the marine equipment the producers needed. His son John, a "real life" beachcomber who is now a producer with the *Stargate* television series, was the official water stuntman, doubling for all of the characters, including Molly.

There were many heavy hearts when the series ended in 1990. According to Gwen Edmonds, current owner of Molly's Reach restaurant, tourists from Germany, Japan, and Australia still come to see the place where the show was produced.

In 1992 Stephen King's *Needful Things* was filmed in Gibsons and once again the town benefited. The Elphinstone Pioneer Museum was given a facelift, and carpenters were hired to build a mock church overtop of the Information Building near Pioneer Park. The Needful Things Store was constructed on Inglis Park and a false front was built over the old Inglis house.

Since the *Needful Things* production ended, only smaller films have been produced on the coast. "There's a big circle on the map of Vancouver," explains Dan Crosby, who is the main provider of marine support for film crews in Vancouver. "Once you get out of that zone, you have to start paying more money to the crew." The Sunshine Coast is unfortunately outside of that circle.

Nevertheless, Soapbox Productions is planning a pilot segment of a "new" *Beachcombers* series and may film it in Gibsons. Conchita Harding, Gibsons' liaison with the BC Film Commission, is constantly working with Tourism B.C. to find ways of encouraging film companies to come here. When they do, she says, "We will be here to welcome them and work with them."

8

A Place Where the Theatre Thrives

The story of the Heritage Playhouse is loosely woven with the development of live theatre on the Sunshine Coast. It began in 1929 when the Gibsons Dramatic Club began staging their productions at the newly-built Women's Institute Hall. Unfortunately, there was not enough space for permanent scenery panels and use of the building gradually declined. During the Second World War it was sold to the school board for one dollar and was used as a gymnasium, then later as a maintenance building.

In the late 1960s Eileen Glassford, a teacher at Elphinstone Secondary, helped form the Driftwood Players. When casting for their first production *Poole's Paradise* began in 1969, Eileen coaxed Nest Lewis, a recent immigrant from Wales, to join the group. Nest had specialized in costumes at university, but with Driftwood she ended up taking a lead role as well as making costumes.

Although that play, and those that followed it were a success, they were always held in gymnasiums or halls where the scenery had to be reconstructed for every performance. By 1988 Nest was fed up with this tiresome task. That's when Fred Inglis asked her to help him find a way to salvage the former Women's Institute Hall by turning it into a theatre. Fred is a great, great grandson of George Gibson, and a grandson of Doctor Frederick Inglis, the Sunshine Coast's pioneer doctor. Active in local theatre since high school, he was also president of the Gibsons Landing Heritage Society, a dedicated group of people committed to saving and preserving local historical buildings. When he discovered that the old hall was about to be demolished, he knew he had to do something to save it.

Fred had drawn plans to show how the building could be turned into a theatre. The first step was a swap with the school board of the Henry Road property, owned by the Town of Gibsons, for the institute property. The town then leased the institute to the Driftwood Players.

Although the building was condemned, Driftwood Players were allowed six months' use of it for fund-raising productions on the condition that firemen

After years of fund-raising and hard work by the Gibsons Landing Heritage Society, the Women's Institute Hall, built in 1929, was transformed into the 150-seat Heritage Playhouse theatre.

were present at every performance. Nest and the other Driftwood Players put on two major plays, *Living Together* and *Steel Magnolias*, but the amount they raised was a pittance compared to what was needed to make the necessary structural repairs. It wasn't until they received a large grant from the B.C. Heritage Trust Fund in 1993 that real change became possible and the reconstruction got underway.

"We saved so much from the original building," says Nest. "The hardwood floors, the wainscoting, even bits of walls covered with mysterious lipstick kisses, which we cut out and put in the washrooms as montages."

While the Society was working hard, it was difficult to show the public what it was doing because the building still looked the same from the outside. Smaller grants enabled them to do a few jobs at a time, but getting those grants proved more and more difficult. "Then," says Nest, "Colleen Elsen came on board. We appointed her Project Director, and with a very astute business plan, she sent off grant applications in every direction." The results were two major grants from the provincial and federal millennium programs, and many local contributions. With generous interim financing by the Sunshine Coast Credit Union, the rebuilding was completed and the Heritage Playhouse officially opened on April 29, 2000. A month later the Driftwood Players

Movie Theatres

The first theatre on the Sunshine Coast operated from the old Union Steamships' dance pavilion in Sechelt, which Morgan Thompson and Bill Parsons had purchased in 1954. Although they sold the building to John Hayes in 1963, the theatre continued until 1971 when it was severely damaged by fire.

Mike Jackson sponsored the construction of the Twilight Theatre in Gibsons. Its 1963 opening feature was *The Pajama Game*. Pamela and Raymond Boothroyd managed—and later owned—the theatre from 1965 till 1995. In those years it was also used for dance classes, Countryside Concerts, and music and dance festivals, often at no charge to the performers. "The Poppy Family performed there before they became famous," says Pamela. "They slept behind the stage because they couldn't afford a motel room. We put curtains around the foyer for them. In the morning they'd come over to our trailer and have breakfast with us."

The Raven's Cry Theatre of the Performing Arts was opened in 1991 as part of the Sechelt Indian Band's House of Hewhiwus. While preference is given to live engagements, which have included Driftwood Players productions, choir groups, the community orchestra, and Coast Recital Society programs, the 274-seat theatre is also equipped with a full-sized movie screen where the latest movies are shown.

To find out what's happening at the theatres call the movie line at 604-886-6843 or the Arts Hotline at 604-886-4278.

Twilight Theatre, May 1972.

*Students from the Sunshine Coast Academy of Dance perform
at the annual Elves Club Telethon. Owned by
Lucy Ennis since 1993, the Academy has over 200 students.*

presented *Arsenic & Old Lace*, in which Nest and Colleen gave first-class performances as Martha and Abby Brewster.

"I dearly want to see this place open every night," says Nest, pointing to the comfortable, raised seating rescued from the old Starlight Cinema in Vancouver. She would like to have a variety of programs developed for all age groups. An arrangement has been made already with the school board to use the theatre as a classroom where students can learn all aspects of drama, "from the writing to the lighting."

Nest believes there are so many talented people on the Sunshine Coast that there will never be a problem finding casts to put on performances. "There are a lot of hard-working, supportive people here: Some very knowledgeable design and technical people and retired or semi-retired professionals who are always willing to give their expertise. And," she adds emphatically, "a very generous business community that supports performances by doing ads and all that sort of thing."

For information on current productions, participation in theatre groups or improvisation nights, contact the Heritage Playhouse at 604-886-8998.

9

A Place of Museums

For people who love the musty trappings of history, the Sunshine Coast offers four uniquely different museums. The oldest repository began as a collection of local artifacts in the basement of Lester Peterson's home on Abbs Road in Gibsons. By 1965 the collection had grown so big that Lester's wife was having a hard time keeping the basement clean. A meeting was held for people interested in establishing a proper museum, and the Elphinstone Pioneer Museum Society was formed. Permission was given to use the basement section of the new Municipal Hall on South Fletcher Road, and the museum was formally opened on May 25, 1965. When this space was needed for a Magistrates Court, the museum was moved to the basement of the adjacent Library Building, and later to Winn Road, which was more accessible to the public.

Included in the museum's large collection is a lantern similar to one that old George Gibson carried down to the dock to meet steamboats arriving after dark, a plough once used to turn sod by pioneer farmers such as Herb Steinbrunner, the rowboat Herbert Evans built from driftwood on his beach, and a newspaper morgue that dates back to copies of the 1945 *Sunshine Coast News*. Nor is the museum limited to human artifacts. A shell collection donated by Charles Bradford features sea treasures from all over the world, and the mineral display provides real examples of copper and nickel ores, crystals, and other geological wonders. Most recently local dentist Don Bland donated his tropical butterfly collection, adding still another dimension to the museum. A hands-on display for children is currently being developed.

From 1989 to1999 Lola Westell worked at the museum, first as president of the society and then as a volunteer curator. Assisted by volunteers and occasionally paid employees, she and her husband Jim organized and indexed the archival records, including more than 4,000 photographs, often using their own funds to travel to Vancouver or Victoria to trace the history of a particular item. Lola was also instrumental in starting the museum's oral history

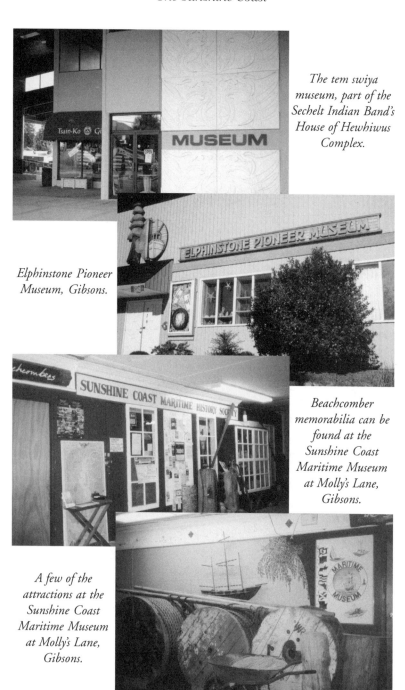

The tem swiya museum, part of the Sechelt Indian Band's House of Hewhiwus Complex.

Elphinstone Pioneer Museum, Gibsons.

Beachcomber memorabilia can be found at the Sunshine Coast Maritime Museum at Molly's Lane, Gibsons.

A few of the attractions at the Sunshine Coast Maritime Museum at Molly's Lane, Gibsons.

project which has tape-recorded histories from seniors who were either born on the coast or came here in the early years of the last century.

When Lola retired, Gail Lewis was hired to manage the museum. Helped by the continued support of dedicated volunteers she has developed a hands-on display for children and special events such as the April 2001 Heritage Play Day, which introduced more than a hundred children to "old time play actitivies."

While winter hours are limited to three afternoons each week, the museum is open five days a week from May to September.

In 1986 the Sunshine Coast Maritime History Society was formed to build a full-sized replica of Captain George Vancouver's ship *Discovery* for the 1992 bi-centennial celebration of Captain Vancouver's British Columbia voyage. When the society was unable to raise the funds necessary to build the ship, they turned instead to establishing the Sunshine Coast Maritime Museum. Located in Molly's Lane, the museum has a large collection of memorabilia from the CBC series *The Beachcombers*, including a life-sized statue of Relic's grandfather, as well as old historic maps, inboard and outboard engines, west coast tugboat artifacts, and a large collection of model ships. Their latest acquisition is the *Persephone* that Bruno Gerussi (aka Nick) used in *The Beachcombers*.

Every summer the Society hosts special events such as a Maritime Weekend. In 1999 they helped organize a visit from the International Retired Tugboat Association, which brought more than twenty old tugboats into Gibsons Harbour.

Managed by an elected board of directors, the museum is operated by volunteers and through student employment grants. Summer hours are Tuesday through Saturday from 10:00 a.m. until 6:00 p.m.

In 1991 the Sechelt Indian Band opened the tem swiya[4] museum in Sechelt. It holds a collection of aboriginal artifacts, including a two-thousand-year-old soapstone carving of a human figure, intricately woven baskets and a full-sized dugout canoe that was made in Egmont around 1915. Museum admission is by donation and guided tours are available for a fee. At the Tsain-Ko Gift Shop next door, Fran Nahanee offers cultural workshops on subjects such as medicine plants, the medicine wheel, and drum making.

The Sechelt Community Archives, which can be accessed at the Sechelt Public Library, also has a small collection of artifacts. Much of the material was assembled by the late Helen Dawe and donated to the people of Sechelt by her sister, Billie Steele.

The most recent addition to the coast's list of museums is located in the chapel of the former St. Mary's Hospital in Garden Bay, which is now the Sundowner Inn. Consecrated by Canon Alan Greene in 1940, the chapel was the scene of many weddings and christenings of Pender Harbour residents

An Ancient Artifact

In 1990 a team of archaeologists was hired to scan the site of a proposed natural gas pipeline. Among their discoveries was a 3,000-year-old stone tool cache found near the Sechelt Food Bank, and a shell midden on the first hill west of Sechelt. One day, as the group was walking over the midden, archaeologist Brad Smart picked up an ordinary-looking rock and suddenly realized it was something special. Later studies showed it to be a 2,000-year-old dish from the Marpole culture that existed 2,500 to 1,500 years ago. Roughly chipped from hardened lava, the grey-brown bowl once had a head, body, tail, and wings on either side. It was used as a grinding bowl, possibly in shamanistic ceremonies. The most unique part of the artifact is that it was the first evidence of Marpole culture to be found in this area, and the only sculpture of this type that has been found in its original location.

Presented to the Sechelt Indian Band, the bowl now resides at the tem swiya museum.

before the hospital closed in September 1974. Managed by Anne Read, one of the Sundowner owners, the museum was only opened in 2000 and artifacts are currently limited to hospital and surgical equipment and a few household and nautical items. Because it is part of the Inn's complex, the museum is open to the public seven days a week.

Elphinstone Pioneer Museum	*604-886-8232*
Maritime Museum	*604-886-4114*
tem swiya museum	*604-885-8991*
Sundowner Inn Museum	*604-883-9676*

10

A Place to Worship

Although there are more than 22 different denominations offering services on the Sunshine Coast today, in 1862 there was only one small chapel built by the Sechelt First Nation at their winter gathering place in Pender Harbour. Four years later the Oblate missionaries persuaded them to erect a church at a place the Sechelts called "Ch'atelich." Longhouses were constructed nearby and whenever the Oblate fathers would visit, the four tribes that make up the Sechelt Nation assembled at this spot. When the church was destroyed by fire (like many buildings of that era that were heated with wood-burning stoves) a new one was built with milled lumber from New Westminster, paid for by a six-dollar levy from each family. Named the Church of the Holy Redeemer, it was opened on April 15, 1873.

One of the most ornate churches on the coast was Our Lady of the Rosary, an imposing twin-spired structure with 2,240 square feet of floor space. It was opened in 1890 amid elaborate celebrations that brought visitors from as far away as the Chilcotin and was reported in great detail in lower mainland newspapers. When it burned to the ground in 1906, the Sechelts built a single-spired church, which was used until it, too, was destroyed by fire on October 25, 1970. Three years later a church on the RCAF base in Ladner was purchased and transported to Sechelt by barge, to become the present Our Lady of the Lourdes church.

Initially non-native Catholics worshipped with the Sechelts. According to the late W. J. "Jack" Mayne, the church would be packed with people and the sermon preached first in Chinook and then in heavily accented English that no one could understand. In 1942 the non-natives opened the Holy Family Church on Cowrie Street. It was consecrated in 1946, the same year that St. Mary's Catholic Church was built in Gibsons.

When he first moved to Howe Sound, George Gibson—although a staunch Methodist—held interdenominational services in his dining room and

Our Lady of the Lourdes Church.

encouraged ministers from Vancouver to visit. As soon as the Gibsons Landing Elementary School was built, the Methodists began using it for Sunday services. Violet Winegarden, the widow of the Gibsons' grandson Ted said, "Mr. Gibson used to go around with his horse and buggy and collect all the children to go to Sunday school, whether the parents liked it or not. The children had to be ready and clean and in their best Sunday clothes." After Charlotte died, George donated land beside the family cemetery for a Methodist church.

In 1905 John Antle, an Anglican Minister from Newfoundland, started the Columbia Coast Mission. One of their first calls was at the Merry Island lighthouse in Halfmoon Bay. For many early settlers of the Sunshine Coast, especially those living at Pender Harbour, Antle and his fellow missionaries became a lifeline to the outside world. As well as offering church services and conducting weddings, christenings, and funerals, these seafaring clergymen brought library books, music (via an organ kept on board the ship), and medical aid. In 1930 they established the first hospital on the Sunshine Coast, a twelve-bed facility at Garden Bay dedicated to Saint Mary. The Rogers family, in memory of Ernest T. Rogers who drowned off Cape Cockburn, donated a bell to the hospital chapel in 1939.

The Story of St. Bart's

At the corner of Highway 101 and North Road is Gibsons' oldest church, known locally as "St. Bart's." It originated in 1892 when an Anglican nun Sister Frances Dalrymple Redmond began campaigning for a church. Land was donated by the Hyde family as a memorial to their son Arthur, and volunteers built a chapel that was dedicated to St. Bartholomew. There was no resident priest, however, and use of the chapel declined when the Columbia Coast Mission boats began calling in at Gibsons in 1905, offering services closer to the waterfront.

For many years the little building, half hidden by trees, was used to store feed and as a shelter for cattle. It was finally restored in 1928 and later a rectory was added. In 1964 St. Bart's amalgamated with St. Aidan's in Roberts Creek and the latter's bell, which had come from the Union Steamship's *Lady Evelyn* (scrapped in 1936), was added to St. Bart's belfry.

An after-school day-care was established at St. Bart's hall in 1993 by the non-profit 937 Daycare Society. Each September they sponsor a Children's Festival at the church that includes storytelling by members of the Sechelt Indian Band, artist workshops, a presentation from Science World in Vancouver, and a children's concert by local musicians.

Construction of St. Bart's present church also began in 1993, and the old chapel was incorporated into the new building. The original beams, complete with axe marks, are still visible. Called the Bethlehem Chapel because of its history of sheltering cattle, it continues to be used for small services and weddings. Across the street is the Gibsons Heritage School, built in 1910 (see below in the background).

Alan Greene, first-born son of Canon Alan Greene, stands beside the
Chelsea II, *which was launched in 1957 as the Columbia Coast Mission's*
John Antle 5. *Skippered by T. Williams and Canon Greene, the vessel*
served as an ambulance, church, and funeral parlour for isolated
communities between Pender Harbour and Whaletown.

In Michael L. Hadley's book, *God's Little Ships: A History of the Columbia*
Coast Mission, Reverend T.A. Lane Connold, M.D. describes a mid-1930s
church service at the hospital:

"[It was] so unlike the regulation Church Service as to have an interest of
its own. The Church is in a hospital ward. Some of the congregation come in
boats and some are in bed. It may be no change for some clergy to know their
congregation are abed, but odd to have them in bed and in Church at one and
the same time. There is no choir. A nurse plays the organ in the sun porch. We
stand to pray and sit to sing for the sake of the infirm. The service is always
liable to interruption because the preacher may be required to sew up a wound
or tap a wheezing chest. There are no collections; and one can come to Church
in pyjamas and dressing gown, or shorts and sea boots as desired."

The United Church also operated a coastal mission and the Reverend
George Pringle would often come to settlements such as Davis Bay and Pender
Harbour on the vessel *Sky Pilot*. In her oral history taped for the Elphinstone

Pioneer Museum collection, Cledia Duncan said, "He used to go up the coast and on the way down he'd notify us at school to tell our parents we were going to have a service in the school on a certain day and all the community used to come to the church service. Just once in a great while."

St. Mary's Hospital in Pender Harbour was closed when the present St. Mary's Hospital was opened in Sechelt in 1964. Every two years, however, a Mission Boat Rendezvous is held at Garden Bay, bringing together the old boats of the Columbia Coast Mission as part of the community's annual Hospital Days event.

As the population of the Sunshine Coast increased, so did the number of permanent churches. Many of these buildings still exist, although some are being used for other purposes such as the old St. Aidan's Anglican Church, built near Hall Road in Roberts Creek in 1936, and the United Church in Roberts Creek, which held its first wedding in 1953 when Harry Roberts' daughter Zoe married Norman Earl from Earls Cove.

Other churches were transferred from one congregation to another. The little white church in Davis Bay with its circular stained glass window was built in 1945 as an interdenominational church, and then served as the St. John's United Church from 1954 to 1982, when it was sold to the Evangelical Lutheran congregation.

St. Hilda's Anglican Church was built beside a cemetery that had been donated by Thomas John Cook when a gravesite was needed for baby Regnheld Evelyn Davidson who died at Doriston in 1923. The cemetery was closed in 1955, and 30 years later the old church was torn down and replaced with a larger facility. Wood from the original structure was used for the pulpits and to panel the rector's office. A new tower was constructed for the bell that had been obtained from St. Mary's Hospital in Pender Harbour in 1973. Recently a garden of remembrance was created near the narthex.

Canon Greene built the smallest church on the Sunshine Coast in Halfmoon Bay after his retirement from the Columbia Coast Mission in 1962. The Church of St. Columba is a tiny A-frame with a maximum seating of seven pews. Above the front door is a carved inscription, "The Church of His Presence." Although privately owned by the Hourigan family, the Anglican Catholic Church is currently renting the building.

Sechelt's first school was opened in one of Bert Whitaker's waterfront buildings in 1912. When he evicted them six months later students were forced to attend classes in the Yamamoto Boat Works, a building that had been used by Japanese fishermen for boat repairs. When the tide came in, the children could see the water through cracks in the floor.

Sechelt Consolidated School opened in March 1939, pictured here before a wing was added on the south end.

11

Schools on the Sunshine Coast

Most schools on the Sunshine Coast fall under the jurisdiction of School District No. 46, which was established in 1946. There are ten elementary schools; three secondary schools located in Gibsons, Sechelt, and Pender Harbour; and a Pathfinder Program that includes six learning centres providing a wide range of independent programs for students who are unable to attend regular elementary or secondary classes. The District has also worked closely with the Sechelt branch of Capilano College to develop a learning centre that offers college-credit courses to senior secondary students.

The success of the district's education program was evident in 1998–99 when Sunshine Coast graduate students won the highest proportion of provincial scholarships in British Columbia. The following spring two students from Pender Harbour won the top prize in environmental sciences at the Canada-wide Science Fair in London, Ontario.

Committed to accepting direction and support from its electorate, the school board and superintendent actively encourage parent and community involvement in the schools, and support both individual Parent Advisory Councils and the Sunshine Coast District Parent Advisory Council. They have also extended financial and promotional support for the Parent Conference organized each year by a group called the Coastal Parents Actively Sharing (C-PAS).

Francophone students on the coast fall under the jurisdiction of School District No. 93 (Conseil scolaire francophone de la C B), with schools located at the Sechelt Elementary and Chatelech Secondary campuses. There are also two independent Christian schools, as well as summer arts and music schools in Gibsons, Roberts Creek, Sechelt, and Pender Harbour. A branch of Capilano College is situated in Sechelt and offers a range of upgrading, university transfer, and career programming courses for residents of the Sunshine Coast. In 1992 the Sea to Sky Outdoor School was started by secondary school teacher Tim Turner to provide "sustainability education." Courses lasting from three to

Sechelt's Residential School

In 1904 the Sechelt native community opened the three-storey St. Augustine's Residential School they had built near the present House of Hewhiwus. It was funded by the Department of Indian Affairs and through the sale of students' needlework, basket weaving, and other crafts. For four and a half hours each day students learned the same subjects taught in public schools. In addition the students looked after a one and a half-acre garden, two cows, and a hundred fowls. While the girls cooked, mended, sewed, and made lace and baskets, the boys worked at milking, carpentry, shoe repairing, fishnet making, woodcarving, and general maintenance.

Not all of the native people of Sechelt were in favour of the boarding school. On July 11, 1916, Thomas John Cook, who was the Justice of the Peace in Sechelt, received a complaint from the mother superior "of insubordination and running away from school of both boys and girls." Justice Cook's response was to have the truants arrested and taken back to the school where all of the children were gathered in an assembly. "I severely lectured them," he recorded in his trial notebook, "and read the sections of the Indian Act regarding the law, and told them all to tell their parents that their conduct would not be tolerated and in future would be punished as directed by the law."

Children who lived close to the school were allowed to go home on Sundays for a couple of hours, and parents were permitted to visit them at the school, but these visits were supervised by one of the nuns and had to be conducted in English. The Sechelt language was forbidden even though many of the children, such as Sechelt elder and historian Gilbert Joe, spoke no English when they were enrolled.

"We were punished if we spoke our language," says Sechelt elder Theresa Jeffries. "Soap in the mouth, slap on the head or arms. We were told we were nothing but savages, that's all we'd ever be."

"But we still yakked," chuckled the late Sechelt elder Joe Paul in a 1990 interview.[5] In a more serious tone he added, "I stayed in grade eight three years because I couldn't get out till I was sixteen."

Although he believes that the residential schools were ethically wrong and used as a manipulative tool by the Department of Indian Affairs, former Sechelt Chief Stan Dixon says he learned valuable lessons there. "The reverend brothers taught us to be polite and respectful of others ... to believe in God, self-discipline, positive behaviour, punctuality, and self-respect, which were all the basic principles of maturity."

In 1912 Ada Dawe (née Cook) attended a Christmas concert at the school. "There was the usual tree, the Indian band played, and all the students participated in singing carols, reciting poems, and performing the little tableaux so popular at that time," reported her daughter, Helen Dawe, in a 1979 *Peninsula Times* article. "Refreshments were served, after which the guests proceeded home on foot, their way lit by coal oil lanterns."

On February 23, 1953 the Sechelt Indian Village day school was opened, giving native students another option besides the residential school. Twenty years later, Clarence Joe was advocating getting native children into public schools. "Why should we be segregated?" he asked in a *Peninsula Times* article of June 6, 1973. "We have gone a long way in a short time. More of our people will soon be active in this community." Within two years band students were fully integrated into School District No. 46 classrooms and the village day school was closed.

In 1985 University of British Columbia Professor Ronald Beaumont published, *She Shashishalhem - The Sechelt Language*. As a result, the Shashishalhem language was soon being taught to the band's nursery school students, and native studies and language programs were developed for those in elementary and secondary school. More recently a Sechelt Indian Band Education Advisory Committee was established with School District No. 46 in an effort to involve the band in decisions about the education of their children, including the most effective way of using federal funding targeted for aboriginal programs.

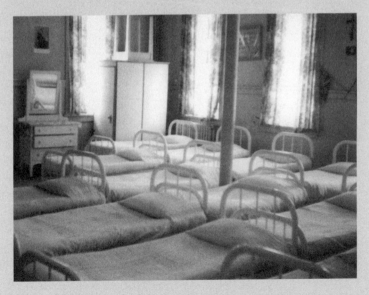

Boy's dormitory, St. Augustine's Residential School, Sechelt, 1966.

five days are held on Keats Island and are offered to schools from Whistler to Tacoma, Washington. "Since 1992," says Tim, "we have offered over two hundred programs to fifteen thousand students. It's all about giving students the knowledge, skills, values, and attitudes needed for life in the twenty-first century. It basically looks at how less is more and how the human enterprise needs to be redirected so that it lives within the means of nature."

All of this is a far cry from the rugged, one-room schoolhouses that the Sunshine Coast's pioneer children attended. Sometimes, they didn't even have a building. At Howe Sound in 1888 Mrs. Henry Smith began teaching some of the new settlement's children in her home. It was two years before the Howe Sound School District was organized and a temporary log cabin school was built on the Gibson property near the waterfront. By the following January a proper school was constructed on a half-acre site obtained from the Aslett pre-emption, and among the children attending were Lottie, Emma, and Hattie Gibson.

In 1910 the two-room Gibson's Landing Elementary School was built on the same property, and the old building was used for high school classes. According to Pearle Tretheway (née Chamberlin), who was enrolled in 1917, teachers hired at the school were not always committed to the standard curriculum. "Mr. Dunbar," she said, "was a man very well versed in languages. Every phrase that came up in English he would tell us what it would be in Greek and write it on the board." Before Pearle graduated, two more rooms had been added to the elementary building. Recently renovated as a heritage site, it now houses the Gibsons Alternate School. Behind it is the modern Gibsons Elementary School with sixteen classrooms, while just up the hill is the Elphinstone Secondary School.

A group of Roberts Creek residents, led by Harry Roberts, built the East Roberts Creek School in 1919 at the corner of Highway 101 and Orange Road. At the same time another group petitioned the government to build the Elphinstone Bay School at what is now the corner of Highway 101 and Lockyer Road. Since the two buildings were less than five kilometres apart and settlement at this time was still sparse, Elphinstone Bay residents had to enrol their pre-schoolers as six-year-olds to make up the number of registrants they needed to qualify for a teacher. The controversy, however, didn't stop Creekers from using that facility for fall exhibitions, community sports days, socials, and lively political debates. Today the Roberts Creek Community School located on Roberts Creek Road continues to be a place shared by the whole community.

In 1912 Herbert Whitaker was persuaded to lend one of his former bunkhouses on the Trail Bay Boulevard for a school. Six months later, he

The third Gibson's Landing Elementary School. Built in 1910, it was recently renovated and designated as a heritge building.

rescinded the offer because he found he could earn seven dollars a month by renting the bunkhouse for a telegraph office. Students then attended classes at an old Japanese boatworks building at the head of Porpoise Bay. Drafty and difficult to heat, the classroom was also very damp because the tides came up under the floor. Fortunately, it was used for little more than a year before an alternative building was found on Wharf Street near its present junction with Inlet Avenue.

During the 1920s the Wharf Street school closed, but two others opened, one at Wilson Creek and one just above Nickerson Road in West Sechelt. In an unpublished manuscript by Helen Dawe, a former student describes West Sechelt's outhouse:

"The son of a prominent Sechelt family was bullied by his schoolmates and got his head stuck down the toilet–a birds eye view of hell, one could call it. That old privy was known as 'The House of Quality.' It reeked of chlorinate of lime. There was never any toilet paper supplied, just old movie books–'Ranch Romances' and good old Eaton's and Simpsons' large catalogues. By Christmas we'd usually reached the hardware section and the paper was hard and shiny."

When attendance at Wilson Creek was too low to keep the school open, students either went to Elphinstone Bay or paid five dollars a month to attend classes with Mrs. Norah Cawley who ran the Sunset Inn at Selma Park. "It was a proper little classroom," remembered one former student. "Mrs. Cawley had an old Chev car that Roger Green fixed for her, and she'd pick up the kids."

Wilson Creek classes were restarted in 1936 when the Jackson Brothers' booming ground brought more families to the area. Del Gilbert began teaching the Sechelt district's first high school courses here. Three years later he was appointed principal of the new Sechelt Consolidated School that replaced the West Sechelt and Wilson Creek facilities, and offered a proper high school program as well as elementary classes.

This building is now part of the Chatelech-Sechelt Community School complex. There are also modern elementary schools at West Sechelt, Davis Bay, and near Kinnikinnick Park.

The Halfmoon Bay School was started in 1915 for the children living in Oscar Niemi's logging camp. It was located at the site of the present-day Wildlife Rehabilitation Centre. "Kids came and went," says Pearle Tretheway, who taught in the school. "I usually had around 25 students from grade one to eight." Pearle boarded with Sarah and Thomas Wall who lived on the Trout Lake Road. "Mr. Wall would go to the school ahead of me to sweep and dust and see that the fire was going. He'd pack the water in—we just had buckets." Wall's daughter, Pat Ness, remembered her mother using a scrubbing board to wash the teacher's clothes.

In 1990 the modern Halfmoon Bay Elementary School was built on Northwood Road, and six years later it became the first community school on the Sunshine Coast.

At Irvines Landing a converted bunkhouse was used as a school from 1920 to 1931 when a new building was erected immediately below a steep cliff. Jean Whitaker, who taught there in the early 1940s, remembers a visiting inspector remarking that it was an awful place to put a school. "That rock is going to come down one day," he warned. In 1942 Robina "Ruby" Ross, a niece of Bertrand Sinclair, came to teach at Irvines Landing. "All of the children came to school by boat," says her daughter Merillee Spearing, who used to accompany her mother to the classroom. She told of one day in the spring of 1944 when rocks began raining down on the roof. The children's parents and relatives came rushing to the landing and up the hill to the school. The teacher hurried all of the children outside, and they met the parents halfway down to the landing. Neither children, teacher, or building were hurt, but it was decided to construct a new school two miles away.

Today the Pender Harbour Community School includes both an elementary school at Madeira Park, and a secondary facility on Highway 101 near Lions Park.

12

Horticulture on the Sunshine Coast

Farming has never been a significant part of the Sunshine Coast's economy, but since the first European settlers arrived there have been local market gardens and farms producing chickens, sheep, cattle, dairy cows, and even llamas. Today, however, most of the coast's gardening is done for decoration rather than sustenance and landscapers and flower gardeners provide a steady supply of customers for more than a dozen nurseries that exist between Earls Cove and Langdale.

Garden clubs in Gibsons, Roberts Creek, Sechelt, and Pender Harbour provide a range of support activities for their members, from talks by experts to garden tours both on and off the coast. While there is much sharing of perennials, most clubs hold plant sales in the spring and fall. Club members also help care for community gardens and raise funds for the food bank, school playground equipment, and a horticultural bursary.

The Sunshine Coast has the advantage of a mild climate and numerous microclimates, says Sechelt Garden Club president Mary Ellen Johnston, "We can grow things that can't be grown other places if we're careful about where we place them in our gardens." Greg Russell of the Roberts Creek Garden Club adds that the coast has "an ideal environment for an English-style garden." He also notes the climate pockets. "I live near Camp Byng, but up at the cemetery there can be a two-week difference in the growing season because of the cold draft off Mount Elphinstone."

Pender Harbour Garden Club president Patsy Baker notes that her area is between a north and south coast climate. "Gardening here is very diverse because of the rocks, moss, and soil within the rocks. Rarely do you find a flat piece of property. But it's probably the best kind of gardening because you can do lots of ponds and creative things."

In pre-European times, the impenetrable nature of the forest east of Wilson Creek led the Squamish natives who lived in this area to rely heavily on the sea

Palms growing at
Bella Beach Motel
in Davis Bay.

Randie Tame's
greenhouse.

Tomato vines at
the Roosendale
Hydroponic Farms,
Garden Bay.

Crafts, produce,
and preserves are
sold in the summer
at the Saturday
Farmer's Market
in Sechelt.

The Sunshine Coast
is an ideal
environment for
goats and kids (sic).

The Sechelt Community
Garden began in 1994.

It includes a
Friendship Garden
of Flowers, an
orchard, Food Bank
garden, and boxes
where local citizens
on a fixed income or
with limited space at
home can grow their
own produce.

The barn was once
part of Norman
Hough's dairy farm.
Today it has been
incorporated into
the Quality Farm
and Garden Store.

for their livelihood. The Sechelt native people, however, were blessed with more open areas and sparser undergrowth. Their seafood diet was supplemented with a variety of roots, plants, fruits, and herbivorous animals. This reliance on wild foods began to wane after the arrival of the Oblate missionaries when Father Paul Durieu encouraged the people to plant gardens. He showed them how to care for cattle and milk cows, and to drain swampland and plant fruit trees in the fertile soil left behind.

For the Sunshine Coast's early European settlers who were isolated from a regular supply of produce, the success of their farms often meant the difference between hunger and plenty. The gardens of George Gibson Sr. were so fruitful he was soon growing enough produce to market it at a stand near the corner of Main and Hastings in Vancouver. In 1893 he used specially blown glass tubes to send his gigantic rhubarb to the Chicago World's Fair where it won an award. John Corlett, who married Gibson's granddaughter Gertie, was equally successful with his market garden located on the site of the present municipal hall and Holland Park.

Dan Steinbrunner, a son-in-law of Thomas and Charlotte Roberts, supplied fresh vegetables and mutton to campers and residents of Gibsons and Roberts Creek. After suffering numerous losses to his flock from bears and cougars he shifted from sheep to raising beef cattle. Purchasing a herd of wild cattle from a farmer on Bowen Island, he transported them by barge to Roberts Creek. During the unloading they were spooked by a passing boat and stampeded ashore, scattering into the woods. Dan rounded them up and herded them to a part of his homestead that lay between two creeks. By removing the centre planks from logging bridges crossing the creeks, he discouraged the cattle from wandering too far. Dan moved his family to Gibsons in 1902, establishing a new farm at what is now the site of The Poplars Mobile Home Park.

Finnish farmers such as Karl Wiren and his son Wiljo used handlogger's tools to clear huge stumps and roots to create pasture land, and eventually built up a large dairy herd. Wiljo and his cousin Laurie delivered fresh milk to many of the summer residents from Grantham's Landing to Roberts Creek.

The Reeves family pre-empted property next to the Steinbrunner's original homestead in 1908 and were soon growing enough vegetables to sell to summer visitors in Sechelt. Esther "Gertrude" Reeves and her husband Jack became famous at local fairs and the Pacific National Exhibition in Vancouver, for their prize-winning exhibits. For a time Gertrude even produced and marketed, under her own label, four-pound tins of black currant jam.

Herbert Whitaker grew the fruits and vegetables he needed for his Sechelt Hotel guests; whatever was left he sold in his store. When he was forced to

Jack "John" Reeves and Esther "Gertrude" Reeves in front of the fireplace at their home in Roberts Creek, c. 1958.

purchase local produce, the Sechelt hotelier drove a hard bargain. According to Norm Burley, Whitaker once quarrelled with Selma Park farmer, Felix Hughes, over a fifteen cent difference in the price of strawberries Hughes was selling.

In 1913 Jiro "Jim" Konishi and his wife Hanna developed a 32-acre market garden and dairy farm on the west shore of Porpoise Bay. Until Jiro's death in 1939 they provided many Sechelt households with milk and produce and for a short time also owned the Settlers Supply House in Selma Park.

The only major pocket of rich arable land in Pender Harbour was farmed by the Klein family who came to the Sunshine Coast in 1911. Their dairy herd and gardens provided milk and produce for many of the local residents. Today this property is the site of the Roosendale Farms, which supplies most of the Sunshine Coast markets with fresh, hydroponically-grown tomatoes and cucumbers. An interesting account of the Roosen family's battles with fire, wind, floodwaters, and elk while establishing their farm can be found in Frank Roosen's book *Fate and Destiny*, which he self-published in 1991.

A resurgence of farming on the Sunshine Coast occurred in the 1970s as Vietnam war protestors settled on the old homesteads, transforming them into communes. Eventually most of these people drifted back to the cities and the communes were returned to individual ownership. The new settlers who remained can often be found selling their organically-grown produce or hand-crafted wares at fairs and Saturday markets in Gibsons, Roberts Creek, Sechelt, and Pender Harbour.

Peter Light inspects bamboo plants. Part of the "drop-out" culture, Peter moved to a commune at Storm Bay in 1967 with his four-week-old daughter, a three-month supply of groceries, and some tools. Today he grows more than a hundred different varieties of bamboo on rented property at Roberts Creek.

Watch for the annual Garden Festival presented each spring at Rockwood Gardens by the Festival of the Written Arts 604-885-9631. For information about garden clubs on the Sunshine Coast, the Gibsons Beautification Contest, or the Great Garden Photo Contest, contact Quality Farm & Garden Supply Ltd. at 604-886-7527.

13

A Place of Parks

Whether you are into riding a mountain bike along a challenging forest trail, hiking up an alpine path, kicking a soccer ball across a green field, bird watching, swimming, or participating in almost any outdoor activity imaginable, the Sunshine Coast has a park where it can be done. There are few things that those who live here can get more enthused about than saving a wetland, shoreline, or forest from destruction. Volunteers have raised funds and pleaded with government agencies to purchase or designate parks and then volunteered and raised funds once more to turn them into useable recreational areas. As a result there are more than 56 parks on the coast, ranging from small municipal playgrounds to an 88-hectare provincial rainforest, as well as two forestry parks, protected wilderness areas, and inter-linking off-road trails that extend almost unbroken from Langdale to Earls Cove.

One of the oldest recreational sites is Brothers Park in Gibsons, which was started in 1950 when logging contractors Al and George Jackson donated five acres of land that was at one time part of Arthur Hyde's homestead. A further nine acres was purchased in 1958 with a provincial government grant and funds raised in the community, and volunteers, including many from the Kiwanis Club, cleared playing fields. Title to the property was transferred to the Village of Gibsons in 1973.

The forest trails, cleared and built by hundreds of volunteers from school age to seniors, are well used by hikers, bikers, and equestrians. One challenging hike along a series of trails accessed at the upper end of Stewart Road leads to a lookout spot on Elphinstone Mountain and a panoramic view of Georgia Strait, from Vancouver's Point Grey to Nanaimo. A more civilized but also steep hike follows a trail from Esperanza or Bridgeman Street to the summit of Soames Hill, where viewers can look down on Howe Sound and Gibsons Harbour.

Cairn marks the spot on Gower Point where Captain George Vancouver and his crew spent the night of June 15, 1792.

Less energetic hikers might prefer to trek along the picturesque Gower Point Road, which is relatively flat, to the Chaster Park waterfront where they can picnic near the spot on which Captain George Vancouver camped one June night in 1792. In Sechelt the Trail Bay promenade also provides easy walking just above a pebble beach. At nearby Snickett Park granite rock formations provide a sculptured foreground to the blue waters of the Georgia Strait.

Bird watchers cherish many local parks. Since 1971 more than two hundred and seventy species of birds have been sighted and recorded on the Sunshine Coast. The Sechelt Marsh trail circles a pond where a variety of waterfowl swim in search of food, or nest on a small, man-made island. Plants such as salmonberry, water hemlock, cinquefoil, ladyfern, and chickweed have been placed throughout the marsh to attract land birds. The Sechelt Marsh Protection Society maintains this park.

The Sargeant Bay wildlife sanctuary, managed by BC Parks and the Sargeant Bay Society is separated from the ocean beach by a man-made berm. From here visitors can view two diverse environments: an ocean beach and an inland marsh that together attract more than 152 species of birds. A four-kilometre trail leads to a viewing area at Triangle Lake.

Roberts Creek from the breakwater at Beach Esplanade Park.

Wetlands are also being developed at Winegarden Park in Gibsons and behind the Madeira Park post office. Site-specific bird checklists for provincial parks at Porpoise Bay and Sargeant Bay are available from the Sunshine Coast Natural History Society, the British Columbia Wildlife Watch, and BC Parks, Garibaldi/Sunshine District at 604-898-3678.

Vehicle-accessed campsites are available at three locations on the Sunshine Coast. The Roberts Creek Provincial Park, designated on August 20, 1954, has 24 campsites, and although there are no showers or hot running water the campsite is sheltered by tall trees and connects with the inland trail system. Within hiking distance is a provincial day park at the foot of Flume Road. It has a grassy picnic area and an ocean swimming beach. A short walk will also lead to the Sunshine Coast Regional District's Beach Esplanade Park at the mouth of Roberts Creek. Here is another picnic area, driftwood sculptures, and a boardwalk built on top of the breakwater. A short distance south along Highway 101 is Cliff Gilker Regional District Park, which has a playground and playing fields, as well as nature trails that wind around waterfalls and over ravines.

Porpoise Bay Provincial Park, established in 1971, has 84 sites, a cyclist camping area for up to 40 people, showers, flush toilets, sani-station, and an

Summer fun at Katherine Lake Park.

adventure playground. Woodland trails follow the salmon-spawning waters of Angus Creek to its Porpoise Bay estuary where a variety of birds and sea life can be viewed. Reservations are required at this campsite and can be obtained by calling 1-800-689-9025 and quoting Campground #37.

The Katherine Lake Regional District Park along the Garden Bay Road has a limited number of campsites, washroom and shower facilities, and a fresh-water swimming area with a sandy beach. Trails lead past a small stream where painted turtles live in a protected environment.

One of the most spectacular parks on the coast is the Skookumchuck Narrows Provincial Park near Egmont. When the Earls Cove ferry terminal was built in 1952, land around Egmont became more appealing to developers. Afraid that houses would replace their special wilderness area, the local residents began lobbying the provincial government to create a park, but it wasn't until 1957 that 35 hectares were set aside for this purpose, with the boundaries expanded in 1987 to 88 hectares. A two-kilometre hike through a rainforest and past the tranquil waters of Brown Lake brings visitors to the Skookumchuck Rapids. Here tidewater from the Strait of Georgia and Jervis Inlet flows through a narrow passageway to land-locked Sechelt Inlet. The water level from one end of the rapids to the other often exceeds two metres and current speeds can reach more

Annual Davis Bay sandcastle competition.

Interacting with waterfowl at the Sechelt Marsh.

than 30 kilometres per hour. Hair-raising stories have been told about logs that shoot eight feet out of the water and crash down again, of whirlpools that have trapped boats and spun them around and around, and of boats thrown onto rocky shores where they were smashed into splinters. Almost as interesting as the rapids is the marine life that can be viewed at low tide on the shores of the Skookumchuck at Roland Point. Here colourful sea stars, plumose anemones, and sea urchins dwell among the granite outcroppings and kelp.

The most recent addition to the Sunshine Coast provincial park system is located at Francis Point near Garden Bay. With a long intricate shoreline marked by rocky cliffs, windswept pines, and twisting arbutus clinging to mossy ledges, this 70-hectare property is home to more than 50 types of moss and six hundred-year-old trees. The

Gnome house and other Terry Chapman carvings can be found along the Chapman Creek Trail accessed at Brookmam Park.

water in front of the park is a favourite dive spot because of its rich variety of sea life. "It's one of the most beautiful places on the Sunshine Coast," says Howard White. He used to play on the property as a youngster, and he has been the tireless leader of an enthusiastic group of local people who put in the hours and energy needed to persuade government leaders, Forest Renewal B.C., the Nature Conservancy of Canada, the Nature Trust of B.C., the Paul G. Allen Foundation, and hundreds of private sponsors to approve and fund the purchase of this property.

There are other places that Howard would like to see turned into parks, such as the Harry Roberts homestead at Cape Cockburn, and the Sechelt Inlet Trail. "I'd love the Sunshine Coast to be known to the world as the 'Place of Parks,'" he says. His big dream is a linked park system that extends from Vancouver to Desolation Sound. "It would be a world attraction on the scale of the West Coast Trail."

With the dedication of the Sunshine Coast people to preserve their natural environment, it's a dream that will undoubtedly become a reality.

14

Youth Camps on the Sunshine Coast

The Sunshine Coast's abundance of breathtakingly beautiful wilderness land, and its close proximity to Vancouver make it an ideal spot for summer camps. An abundance of trees enables lodges and cabins to be secluded in separate clusters, and allows campers to feel alone with nature even on a day when there are more than 250 children and adults in residence. Most of the institutions running the camps are dedicated to keeping their property as close to its natural state as possible. Built on the waterfront, they offer a range of activities from snorkelling, kayaking, and sailing; to learning outdoor living skills, archery, and rock climbing; as well as sports such as volleyball, basketball, and tennis; and indoor and outdoor craft programs. During the off season the camps are often rented by schools and community or church groups for nature studies, recreation, and retreats.

One of the first youth camps on the coast was started in 1906 when T.H. Hutcheson of the Vancouver YMCA established Camp Elphinstone just north of what is now the Langdale ferry terminal. Today 300 children from all over the world arrive every two weeks for an adventure-filled holiday at this 110-acre camp.

The Kewpie Camp for girls was situated on property purchased in 1919 from Harry Roberts just northeast of the bridge near the mouth of Roberts Creek. Owned and operated by Miss K. Brydon, this camp eventually featured a large dining hall, social hall, several huts, and a private trail to the beach. Campers wore khaki bloomers and long khaki jackets, with red tie and beret as accessories. Their days were filled with outdoor concerts and plays, crafts, swimming, and rowing—and occasionally—forbidden rides down the McNair shingle flume. Often the girls would serenade arriving or departing steamboats in an impromptu chorus on the wharf. Although the camp closed and was sold after Miss Brydon's death, three of the original buildings continue to be used by the current owners, the P.D. O'Brian family.

*The Playhouse—one of the original Kewpie Camp
buildings still in use by the O'Brian family.*

Crowded living conditions in Vancouver's downtown east side during the 1920s led Reverend J. Richmond Craig of the First Presbyterian Church to search for a spot where mothers and children could find some relief from the city during the summer. In 1923 a 65-acre homestead on Gambier Island was purchased for this outreach program and named Camp Fircom after the First Presbyterian Church (which became First United Church in 1925) and the First Community Services. In those days campers rowed to the island, but today they are transported from Vancouver aboard the MV *Kona Winds*, or by water taxi from Horseshoe Bay. Camp facilities include beaches, playing fields, hiking trails, accommodations, and a dining hall and kitchen that can seat up to 120 guests. Unique to the camp are subsidized camps for mothers and their children. For Margaret Gabriel, who now lives on Gambier Island, it allowed her—as a single Mom—to have a summer holiday with her three children that she could never have afforded otherwise.

The Anglican Church's Camp Artaban at Long Bay on Gambier Island began as a summer resort for girls in 1924. Today the camp is open to children, youth, and adults and provides a variety of summer activities.

In the spring of 1922 the Vancouver District Scout Council brought 60 boys to a camp-out on a twice-logged over piece of property known first as Cassidy's Landing and later as Doherty's in Roberts Creek. The scouts were so

The B.C.–Yukon Provincial Jamboree at Camp Byng, 1999.

impressed with the location they planned more camps, and in July they were visited by the Governor-General of Canada, Lord Byng of Vimy. When the Scouts purchased the property in 1925, they called it "Camp Byng" in his honour. Cedar, fir, and hemlock trees have since grown back in abundance, and each summer more than 4,500 boys and girls take part in activities on the 240-acre site. "You meet everyone here from all walks of life," says Scouts Canada representative, Brian Peterson. "Coming here is one thing families can do together."

Discovering that there was no Salvation Army youth camp for the Vancouver area in 1925, S.A. Colonel Arch Layman and Captain Fraser Morrison rowed up and down the coast from Langdale to Gibsons, searching for a place to establish a camp. The property they acquired is located on the south side of the present ferry terminal. For more than 75 years their Camp Sunrise has provided summer programs for underprivileged children. The camp has a cafeteria, chapel, pool and hot tub, as well as a huge field for sports activities.

The Baptist Church purchased Keats Island Camp in 1926. Throughout the summer the Convention of Baptist Churches runs children's camps on the 400-acre site. Besides cabins for children and staff there is a lofted building with a stage, smaller meeting rooms, a mess hall, and a tuck shop. The *Dogwood Princess* passenger ferry at Langdale accesses the island.

Rose Cottage at the Camp Olave Girl Guide Camp was built by the Rat Portage Lumber Company, which logged the area from 1904 to 1907.

With the help of a local farmer George Walker, who provided free advice, labour, and plenty of fresh vegetables, the Girl Guide Camp was established in 1927. Located on the old sorting grounds of the Rat Portage Lumber Company, the camp used many of the original company buildings, including two that remain today: Rose and Brock cottages. Managed by the Camp Olave Management Committee, the camp hosts approximately 5,000 girls each year. So memorable are these outings, says caretaker Pat Beninger, that she frequently has people in their 60s and 70s stopping by to revisit the place they knew as children.

The Union Steamships were still running in 1946 when the Westminster Presbytery purchased Beach Avenue property owned by Frank Norman Raines and created Camp Douglas. Now as many as 1,100 children and adults attend the Presbytery's weekend and summer camps.

Although Princess Louisa Inlet has not been included in the scope of this book, it would be negligent not to mention the Malibu Club, one of the most famous youth camps on the coast. In the mid-1930s Thomas F. Hamilton, a partner in Hamilton Beech Aircraft Ltd., began buying up all the old crown grants surrounding Princess Louisa Inlet and then spent two million dollars to build a resort on the north side of Malibu Rapids. The Malibu Club had its own power plant, nine-hole golf course, and volleyball and tennis courts. Barge loads of sand were brought in to create beaches, and guests had the use of an assortment of boats from canoes to small yachts. Closed after the outbreak of the Second World War, the resort was sold in 1953 to the Young Life Society founded by Jim Rayburn. Today Malibu is run by the society as a Christian high school camp for teenagers from Canada and around the world. Besides a rock swimming pool overlooking the rapids and the thirteen-hole golf course, a variety of other camp activities are available including water skiing, snorkelling, a tower swing, and ropes course. Each week the Young Life's *Malibu Princess* travels from Egmont to Princess Louisa loaded with campers.

Youth Camp Contacts

Camp Artaban Society
1058 Ridgewood Drive, North Vancouver, B.C. V7R 1H8
Phone: 604-980-0391

Camp Byng, Scouts Canada
Vancouver Coast Region, 664 W. Broadway, Vancouver, B.C. V5Z 1G1
Phone: 604-879-5721 Fax: 604-879-5725
E-mail: vcrofficd@vcr-scouts.com

Camp Douglas
RR 22 1341 Margaret Road, Roberts Creek, B.C. V0N 2W2
Phone: 604-885-4493 or the Westminster Presbytery,
604-520-1331 Fax: 604-520-7072
E-mail: info@campdouglas.ca
Website: <www.campdouglas.ca>

Camp Elphinstone, YMCA Outdoor Camping
S7 C-9 RR#1, Port Moody B.C. V3H 3C8
Phone: 604-939-9622 Fax: 604-939-9621
Website: <www.ymca.vancouver.bc.ca>

Camp Fircom Society
320 East Hastings Street, Vancouver, B.C. V6A 1P4
Phone: 604-662-7756 Fax: 604-662-7716
E-mail: info@campfircom.bc.ca

Camp Olave Management Committee, Girl Guides of Canada, B.C. Council
1476 West 8th Ave., Vancouver, B.C. V6H 1E1
Phone: 604-714-6636 Fax: 604-714-6645
Website: <www.bc-girlguides.org>

Camp Sunrise, Salvation Army
4727 E Hastings, Burnaby, B.C. V5C 2K8
Phone: 604-299-3908
Website: <www.nsnews.com/proj/summer99/camp-3.html>

Keats Island Camp, Convention of Baptist Churches
234 Brooksbank, North Vancouver, B.C. V7J 2C1.
Phone: 604-980-6799

Malibu Club
Box 49, 6545 Maple Road, Egmont, B.C. V0N 1N0
Phone: 604-883-2582 Fax: 604-883-2082
E-mail: malibuclub@malibu.younglife.org

15

A Place to Boat

From as early as 1886 when George Gibson sailed his eighteen-foot sloop *Swamp Angel* into what is now Gibsons Harbour, the Sunshine Coast has been known for its wide range of boating opportunities, providing safe havens in stormy weather and challenging seas and white-water rapids for adventurers. While there are winds and currents that are predictable to each small area, sudden squalls can also appear, turning placid waters into white-capped waves in a matter of moments. Every cove and bay has its own unique shoreline, from sandy flats to sheer granite cliffs, and boaters who know the area and the rocks to avoid can often go close to shore without any danger of grounding.

Rugged mountains, clusters of odd-shaped islands, and steep waterfalls form a backdrop to a wildlife paradise. Majestic eagles surfing air currents, Canada geese, Bonaparte gulls, kingfishers, loons, scoters, cormorants, and blue herons share this paradise with black bears, Columbia black-tail deer, river otters, chubby black seals, California sea lions, black and white Orcas, and occasionally a grey whale. Purple and orange starfish cling to sea-worn boulders, rainbow-coloured anemones fasten onto pilings, and jellyfish like unmanned parachutes undulate through the water. In Porpoise Bay and off the mouth of Chapman Creek, coho salmon jump high out of the water, their silvery scales shimmering in the light. Bright red snappers, spiny rock cod, and huge lingcod swim close to the ocean floor in search of food.

From Plumper Cove on Keats Island to Princess Louisa Inlet, rest stops can be made at numerous marine parks, some with pit toilets and campgrounds. For detailed, up-to-date information, contact the BC Parks website at <www.elp.gov.bc.ca> or <www.bigpacific.com>. Old logging roads and trails also invite boaters who wish to stretch their legs to explore inland forests where the occasional old growth fir or cedar can still be found.

Bird sanctuaries have been designated on Christie Islet and Pam Rock in Howe Sound, the White Islets near Davis Bay, and on Franklin Islet just west

How the Inlets were Formed

During the Pleistocene Age glaciers crept down the river valleys of the Sunshine Coast, gouging out the softer sedimentary rock that lay between the folds of granite bedrock. In this way the Jervis River was cut deeper and wider and when the ice retreated, it had become an inlet. It now has the distinction of registering the greatest maximum depth of any of British Columbia's 37 inlets: 2,400 feet or almost half a mile. Its average mid-inlet depth is nearly one-third of a mile: 1,620 feet. At 48 nautical miles from head to mouth, it is also one of the longest of the 37, yet its width rarely exceeds one and a half miles.

The Jervis River's tributary streams—Sechelt River, Salmon River, and Narrows River—which had developed comparatively straight channels because they followed uninterrupted faults in the granite bedrock also became inlets of the sea, though not as deep as Jervis Inlet.

of Halfmoon Bay. While these areas are off-limits to humans, there is an accessible sanctuary at Sargeant Bay, developed by BC Parks and the Sargeant Bay Society. To protect the birds and their habitat, dogs must be kept on a leash in this park.

An increasingly popular way of exploring the coastal waterways is by kayak. *Paddling the Sunshine Coast* by Dorothy and Bodhi Drope is an excellent resource book for these boaters. During their ten years of kayaking the coast prior to writing the book, the Dropes became well acquainted with local winds, currents, and danger zones. They have mapped out trips that can take a couple of hours to several days, and include details of wildlife, sanctuaries, campsites, trails, and facilities. There are also many companies on the coast that rent kayaks and offer guided excursions, including full-moon paddles and interpretive tours. They'll trailer the kayaks to the area their clients wish to explore, and retrieve them when the trip is over.

For boaters who are more interested in action than in sightseeing, the coast has had a long tradition of holding local regattas. In 1929 the first West Howe Sound Annual Regatta was held in Gibsons, and by 1948 they were offering separate girls' and boys' sailing races, fancy diving competitions, races on homemade rafts, canoes and rowboats, and an evening bonfire with community singing and refreshments.

Organized in 1976 to lobby and raise funds for construction of the Gibsons Marina, the Gibsons Yacht Club continues to hold sailing races every Sunday.

*Blind dinghy (above) races and a power dinghy demonstration (below)
are a traditional part of the fun at the annual Hospital Bay
Days celebrations at Pender Harbour.*

The Canoe Challenge

The First Nations of the Sunshine Coast once travelled in canoes that measured from 35 to 70 feet long, made from giant hollowed-out cedar trees; during the 1920s and 1930s the Sechelts' canoes won championship races up and down the northwest coast. The *St. Michael*, a 50-foot war canoe, was hand carved in 1934. The following February the canoe's eleven-man crew started training and by May they were ready to enter the big Nanaimo race. "Right away we took the lead," said the late David Paul in a *Peninsula Times* article by Dick Proctor,[6] "and even though the wind was blowing and the water was rough, we stayed in front. We had practised making turns so that we could turn in 25 to 30 seconds." The paddlers won the race by at least 400 feet. "Nobody else was even close to us."

Today canoes that copy the original native designs are being built using modern techniques and materials, and there is a new interest in the social and healing benefits experienced through the teamwork required to paddle these large boats.

"The canoes are a community," explains Gibsons' Staff Sargeant Ed Hill, who participated in a Vision Quest outrigger canoe journey from Hazelton to Victoria in 1997. "And the canoe doesn't travel unless you all work together."

A few months after the journey Ed was transferred to Gibsons where he soon gathered a team of paddlers, found a loaner canoe, and started practising. By 1999 he and his teammates had helped organize the first Howe Sound Outrigger Iron Race—a Canadian National championship race with a 20-mile course and 25 participating teams. When it was over Gibsons was dubbed as the "Kona of the North," and the Iron Race established as an annual event. The team then organized the Gibsons Paddle Club, which now has over 80 members and its own canoes stationed in Gibsons, Sechelt, Pender Harbour, and Powell River. In 2001 the Iron Race won the B.C. Tourist Attraction award. Outrigger races have also been established in Sechelt and Pender Harbour.

In February 2000 the Sunshine Coast Aboriginal Friendship Centre in partnership with School District No. 46 purchased a 31-foot-long fibreglass canoe, the *Yanke Dene*, which means "people of the earth." Their goals were to enable both native and non-native students to experience the benefits of teamwork, and to study science, natural history, and other disciplines. That summer Friendship Centre president Dan Lindsey and a group of ten teens paddled the canoe between Comox and Victoria as part of Tribal Journey 2000. The journey ended on July 26 in Victoria Harbour where welcoming ceremonies were held by the Songhees and Esquimalt nations.

Local teens in the Yanke Dene, *piloted by Dan Lindsay, return to the Gisbons wharf after attending Tribal Journey 2000, which included twelve days of paddling from Comox to Victoria.*

Gordie Tocher and the Orenda *at the Malaspina Ranch Resort. Tocher and his crew made an epic voyage from Vancouver to Hawaii in this carved replica of a Haida dugout canoe. The outrigger is housed at the West Vancouver Museum.*

At a 10 a.m. skipper's meeting in their clubhouse beside the marina, the course is worked out and crews are selected. According to Fleet Captain David Smethurst, "The ten-mile race gives us three hours of sailing. That usually gets us back in after enough fun on a good day and enough torture on a poor one." Every summer a two-day regatta is held with 30 to 40 boats participating from sailing clubs in Squamish, Bowen Island, Nanaimo, Maple Bay, and in the Vancouver area.

Besides organizing group cruises to places like the Gulf Islands or Desolation Sound, the Gibsons Yacht Club also provides accommodation for the power squadron and coast guard auxiliary's "Pleasure Craft Operator's Certificate Course" and sponsors a "Learn to Sail" program, hiring instructors and providing boats, classroom space, docks, and equipment for the dinghy sailing program. "This year we had three instructors," says David. "The one who specialized in younger children called herself the Director of Web Feet." When they've completed the course the kids are invited to join the club as junior members and to participate in sailing events.

Every Saturday morning the Garden Bay Sailing Club holds races that run from two to four hours. "Sometimes you need to throw salt water on the lines to get the frost off," admits Commodore Tom Barker, "but we race twelve months of the year." Every July since 1989 they have hosted the Malaspina Annual Regatta with races during the day and a barbecue in the evening. "Malaspina Strait has the best wind conditions any regatta has," says Tom. "They're pretty consistent." To encourage young people to start sailing, club members have made two sailing dinghies and offer Canadian Yachting Association White Sail courses for levels one through three to anyone aged ten and older. When they've completed the course the kids are invited to crew on the larger boats during the Saturday morning races.

The Pender Harbour Power Squadron and the Sunshine Coast Power Squadron both offer "safe boating" courses to anyone who wants to be on the water. After successful completion of the introductory course of twelve once-a-week lessons, students obtain a boat operator's certificate and are eligible for further courses in piloting, advanced piloting, navigation, electronics, and boat and engine maintenance. "Everything to help them be a safer boater," says Commander Doris Farrand whose Pender Harbour squadron also organizes group cruises and takes part in the annual Christmas Carol Cruise.

Coast Guard Auxiliary units in Gibsons, Halfmoon Bay, and Pender Harbour handle marine rescue operations on the Sunshine Coast. Calls to the Coast Guard are made to the Canadian Coast Guard Rescue Centre in Victoria (1-800-567-5111) where they will be forwarded to the Sunshine Coast unit that is in the best position to help. Both the Halfmoon Bay and Gibsons units have high speed, rigid hull, inflatable rescue crafts with a Global Positioning System (GPS), radar, depth sounder, and towing winches. Pender Harbour has an owner/operator program in which approximately ten boat owners use their own vessels to help in search and rescue operations. All auxiliary members, including owner/operators must take auxiliary-funded courses in boating safety and first aid and obtain a restricted radio license. At least once a year a combined barbecue and exercise session is held involving as many units as possible, including those from Nanaimo, French Creek, Powell River, and the regular Coast Guard. "We do routine stuff like practising towing people alongside, or transferring an injured person from one vessel to another," says owner/operator Brian Fawkes.

Since 1995 the number of rescue incidents on the Sunshine Coast has declined, largely as a result of Coast Guard Auxiliary Zone Director Ken Moore's efforts to increase marine safety practices. Ken is also Director of Boating Safety for B.C. and the Yukon, and has over two hundred people trained to give free inspections of pleasure boats and to assist their owners and operators in safety guidelines. "We don't just tell them they need life jackets," he says. "We tell them why they should wear personal flotation devices and how to test them." He describes a recent boating accident where the person wearing a life jacket survived while her partner without a life jacket did not. He also encourages people to check their boats before they head out and to obtain a weather forecast. "The weather here can change very quickly," he warns.

If you would like a safety check on your boat, call the Canadian Coast Guard's toll-free number at 1-800-267-6687, or check with your local marina for the number of the nearest Coast Guard Auxiliary unit. The Boater Safety Office number in Victoria is 1-250-480-2792; this number is not toll free.

Cyclists line up for the Poker Challenge race at the annual Mountain Bike Festival in Sechelt (top). Lenarduzzi Soccer Camp, Ted Dixon Memorial Park in Sechelt (middle). Boomstick races are a traditional part of logger sports events at the annual Gibsons Sea Cavalcade (bottom).

16

A Place Where Sports are Celebrated

Breaking away from the defenseman, who's been in his face like an angry hornet, the young soccer forward dribbles the ball towards the goal, searches briefly for backup, and seeing only the defenders crowding in again, gives a mighty kick. The ball soars into the top right corner of the net. It's a goal!

Participating in or watching sports on the Sunshine Coast is a year-round tradition and one that began long before European settlement. In the late 1800s, young Sechelt men risked the wrath of the Oblate missionaries by purchasing a soccer ball and uniforms so they could play the Nanaimos. Discovering that they had both a talent and a passion for the game, the band organized leagues and by the 1950s were playing intertribal games against Musqueam, Squamish, Sliammon and Nanaimo teams. Recent triumphs have included the Xenicen Eagles' winning of the B.C. Supercup n July 2000, participation of five members from the women's team on the B.C. Aboriginal Women's Soccer Team at competitions in Australia in August 2001, and hosting the August 2001 Canadian Aboriginal Youth Soccer Qualifying Games in Sechelt.

Early settlers also enjoyed sports such as badminton, baseball, skating and boating. In a description of the May 24 celebrations during the 1920s and 1930s at Pender Harbour, James Warnock told of a picnic at Point Cockburn: "The boats took a whole load of kids up there … Everybody took about three or four cakes and a big box full of sandwiches and we all fed everybody. We had our races there and our contests."[7] He recalled other celebrations that were held at the Donley's Landing School: "We had about an acre to an acre and a half, a great big field, and we used to run our races there, jumping and playing baseball." On almost every weekend they would have baseball games at the school. Wilfred "Tiffy" Wray mentioned ice-skating on the lakes whenever it was cold enough for the water to freeze. In the 1940s and 1950s, Caryl Cameron and Isabel Gooldrup belonged to badminton leagues. "They used to go to Sechelt and Gibsons to play badminton," says Caryl. " They had to go by boat until the road was built."[8]

"And we used to go up Jervis and play with the [people in] the logging [camps]," adds Isabel. "They just loved to see us. Put on a big spread … we'd start out early in the day and get up there and play badminton half the night and get home in the morning."[9]

Tennis was popular with the summer tourist crowd and during the 1920s and 1930s there were tennis courts at resorts such as the Dunn's Resort in Roberts Creek, and at the Union Steamship picnic sites in Selma Park and Sechelt. The tennis courts at Dougall Park in Gibsons, which were rebuilt in 1952, now host the Annual Gibsons Open Tennis Tournament that was started as a fund-raiser in 1975 by the Elphinstone High School tennis team. For the past five years the tournament has been organized by Karin Tigges, secretary of the Suncoast Racquet Club.

From September to mid-April the Sunshine Coast Arena in Sechelt is open to public skating, figure skating, and hockey. With 17,000 square feet of ice and a 225-person bleacher capacity, the arena also has a skate shop, concession stand, lounge bar, and banquet room. Almost every Thursday, Friday, and Saturday evening commercial men's league games can be watched, and during the playoffs the arena bleachers are full of spectators. In between these competitions are the minor league games arranged by the Sunshine Coast Minor Hockey Association. When hockey is not on the agenda, the Sunshine Coast Skating Club is practising. This group puts on a carnival each February where more than one hundred and sixty young skaters perform. They've also produced champion figure skaters such as nine-year-old Michael Jensen who won the 1999 Jingle Blades competition in White Rock. The club's three coaches teach everything from figure skating to hockey manoeuvres.

The Gibsons Curling Club offers competitive curling from ten-year-olds to seniors. More than 40 teams participate in different leagues, including ten senior's teams, and they frequently have workshops for newcomers. The club is part of the Pacific Coast Curling Zone; their season runs from October 1 to the end of March. In 2001 they hosted the International Tankard competition. The Gibson rink, built in 1974, has no bleachers but there is a viewing area in the upstairs lounge.

Besides school greens, there are eight soccer fields on the coast, including those with night lights at Ted Dixon and Cliff Gilker parks. The soccer season begins in September with the Clarence Joe Jr. Memorial Cup and the Prowave Soccer Camp (formerly the Lenarduzzi Soccer School), and runs until April with a break in December and January to protect the fields. There are eighteen

A Place to Dive

The Sunshine Coast gained importance as a destination for recreational diving after the Artificial Reef Society sank the 367-foot Canadian destroyer *Chaudiere* in Sechelt Inlet in 1992. Resting in 50 to 90 feet of water, the vessel has become a home for hundreds of species of marine life, including invertebrates, fish, and algae. Divers also come to explore the remnants of other vessels such as the *Aliford*, a steam-powered fish packer that burned and sank in 1917 near Nelson Island, and to find relics from logging camps and resorts as well as memorabilia tossed overboard from the Union Steamships.

The remains of the SS *Aliford*. Discovered in 1970 by John Seabrook.

The greatest attraction for Sunshine Coast divers, however, is the variety of sealife that is visible year-round. "It's true emerald sea diving," says Tony Holmes, owner of Suncoast Diving & Water Sports, which offers diving equipment and lessons, waterfront accommodation, and charters. The Skookumchuck Rapids, he adds, is considered "the number one B.C. dive." Here, high oxygen levels cause plants and animals to flourish.

Chris Kluftinger, owner of the Beaver Island Bed and Breakfast, also offers diving charters, and his walls are covered with photographs he's taken of nudibranchs, wolf eels, and other sea creatures. "This is probably the best diving destination that you can reach from Vancouver in a single day," he says. He describes Gorgonian fan corals and gigantic cloud sponges which he compares to delicate, thin-walled sculptures with tubes and bowls and different shapes with holes in them. Hiding inside the holes are juvenile rockfish, crabs, and shrimp.

In his dives Chris has witnessed an eighteen-inch, eel-like creature called a red brotula, and has twice encountered a six-gilled shark, also known as a cow shark. He is quick to point out that there are no dangerous animals in the waters of the Sunshine Coast, but cautions that sea creatures, like other wildlife, have the power to defend themselves when they feel threatened.

men's and women's soccer teams and 82 Sunshine Coast Youth Soccer Association teams.

Rugby is popular in Gibsons where the Gibsons Rugby and Athletic Association has a team made up of players from the whole Sunshine Coast that competes in the Vancouver Rugby Union. Formed in the early 1970s, the club leases their clubhouse from the Town of Gibsons in exchange for the upkeep of Armours Beach.

During the spring and summer ball diamonds from Pender Harbour to Langdale are in constant use by softball and baseball leagues. There are also summer basketball and volleyball camps, as well as beach volleyball, which can be played at courts in Davis Bay and Sechelt.

Throughout the year there are regular activities at the coast's two swimming pools, located in Gibsons and Pender Harbour. The Gibson pool organizes the medal-winning Chinook Swim Club, open to kids from ages six to seventeen, while at Pender Harbour a swim club is just being established.

Martial arts instruction is available at academies in Gibsons and Sechelt, and through the community schools. At the White Tower Park in Gibsons an archery course has been constructed. A skateboard park was opened in 1997 at Chatelech Secondary School. Built by local volunteers, and financed through raffle sales and a large donation from the Rotary Club, the park also contains two paved basketball courts.

The Sunshine Coast Rod and Gun club has a shooting range in Wilson Creek and holds an annual turkey shoot each December with a variety of events from .22-calibre and large-bore rifle shooting to shotgun competitions. They also hold annual hunter training courses and raise money for local conservation causes.

Just up the road from the Rod and Gun club is the Sechelt Airport, which explodes with noise and excitement each summer when the Sunshine Coast Drag Racing Association holds races, bringing competitors from as far afield as Arizona. One event, held in August 2000, drew 160 registered contestants and a crowd of over 5,500 spectators.

Known as the "Golf Coast of Canada," the Sunshine Coast has four unique golf courses. At the Langdale Heights RV Park there is a Par 3 facility, open to the public and free to guests staying at the park, complete with practice green and driving net, and lessons from PGA pro Ken Batchelor.

The Sunshine Coast Golf and Country Club in Roberts Creek created a nine-hole course in 1969 and has now expanded to eighteen holes with a challenging mix of terrain, a clubhouse with a deck overlooking the Straits of Georgia, a golf shop, and CPGA staff to provide group and individual lessons.

A Place to Fish

The Sunshine Coast's best-kept secret is its saltwater and freshwater fishing, which includes having one of the few terminal fisheries for coho salmon in the province. Chinook can be caught year-round, pink salmon are available from July to October, and chum salmon are fished from August to October. Anglers can also catch rock cod and red snappers throughout the year, and there is a limited season for lingcod.

Bob Dixon offers fishing charters through Davis Bay Sports Fishing. Although he's available for full-day charters, he prefers trips that last about four hours. His boat will accommodate two to three people and he provides all the gear needed. In his spare time Bob serves on the board of the Sunshine Coast Salmon Enhancement Society and volunteers at the Chapman Creek hatchery.

Year-round freshwater fishing is available at many easily accessible lakes and creeks on the coast. Cutthroat trout weighing up to five pounds have been caught at Trout, Klein, Waugh, Brown, and Garden Bay Lakes, while at Ruby Lake there is a healthy stock of kokanee and trout. Paq Lake is restricted to catch and release and single barb less hooks.

Scott Elliott runs Trout Tales, a freshwater guiding service. Fully licensed and insured he provides all equipment, lunch, beverages, and transportation for lake, river, creek, and ocean shore fishing.

For the latest information on both ocean and freshwater fishing, check out the Sunshine Coast Sport Fishing website at <www.twineagles.bc.ca/ bcfishing.html>.

In May 2000 the Elphinstone Secondary School golf team, which trains at this club, won the North Shore high school golf championship.

Built in 1993, the Sechelt Golf and Country Club's eighteen-hole course is noted for its wide-open spaces and breath-taking views of the ocean and mountains. It has a full-sized, year-round driving range with covered tees, and CPGA Head Professional Dean Totten provides golf instruction.

Considered one of British Columbia's best nine-hole courses, the Pender Harbour Golf Club is a mountainous course with both gently rolling and hilly fairways. It also has a clubhouse that offers meals and refreshments.

In recent years the coast has hosted championship golfing competitions such as the B.C. Public Links provincial tournament held in May 2000 at Roberts Creek. The first Iron Man Golf Tournament, sponsored by the *Coast Reporter*, was held on April 1, 2001. This 36-hole event, incorporating all four

The Sunshine Coast's Terminal Fishery

A terminal fishery begins at a hatchery, such as the one at Chapman Creek, where eggs are harvested in the fall from returning salmon, then fertilized and incubated in a protected and monitored environment. The hatchlings, or "fry," are then transferred to tanks and nourished until they become smolts and are capable of surviving in salt water. Their adipose fins are clipped so they can be identified as terminal fish, and they are subsequently released into areas where, upon their return in three to five years, they can spawn in the streams and provide a recreational fishery.

As a result of the development of such a fishery by the Sunshine Coast Salmon Enhancement Society increased numbers of coho and chinook salmon are returning to local waters. During the summers and falls of 1999 and 2000, Halfmoon Bay, Porpoise Bay, Davis Bay, and Chapman Creek were among the very few places open to coho fishing in the province.

golf courses, was such a success that planning for the 2002 tournament began as soon as the 2001 tournament was over!

Many local bed and breakfast facilities offer "stay and play" packages with golfing discounts.

Lawn bowling is also available on greens at the Sechelt Golf and Country Club. The Sechelt Lawn Bowling Club runs tournaments with Powell River and West Vancouver clubs, and has regular practice and draw days. Coaching is offered to newcomers and lawn bowls can be rented at the facility.

The only indoor bowling facility on the coast was opened in 1974 by Gail and Bud Mulcaster. The Gibsons Lanes has eight lanes for five-pin games. Although they are closed during July and August, for the rest of the year they have league games, seniors, mixed and public bowling, as well as special Olympic games.

The Sunshine Coast Equestrian Club, the Gibsons Riding Club, and a Back Country Horseman Club organize equestrian events. A large, outdoor riding ring along the B & K logging road in Roberts Creek is the scene of many horse shows and competitions from spring through fall, including the Children's Wish Trail Ride that benefits the Children's Wish Foundation of Canada. Two former members of the Sunshine Coast Equestrian Club, Janine Ellingham and Jodi Orth (née Custance), have gone on to compete with the Canadian Olympic team. Janine frequently returns to the coast to give riding clinics.

Mountain biking and hiking are becoming a major tourist attraction for the coast as more and more back-country trails are developed. Each trail is

Annual April Fools Run begins at Sunnycrest Mall in Gibsons and ends at the House of Hewhiwus in Sechelt (top). Kayakers paddle through the white water of the Skookumchuck Rapids (middle). A rider competes at one of the many horse shows held during the summer on the Sunshine Coast (bottom).

uniquely different, such as the Gnome Trail along Chapman Creek where carvings by Terry Chapman can be found in unexpected niches. In 2000, with the exception of about ten kilometres of highway trekking, it was possible to travel from Langdale to Pender Harbour on inter-linking trails. At an annual Trail-Fest event held in May more than a thousand adults and children spent the weekend clearing and repairing the old trails and constructing new ones.

Slopes for both cross-country and downhill skiing are found in the Tetrahedron and Dakota ridge wilderness areas. In 1987 the Tetrahedron Ski Club and community volunteers, who had already cleared and marked trails through this protected area, also built four cabins and had them airlifted into the park. The Dakota Ridge Winter Recreation Committee, formed in 1996, is working hard to develop this plateau that ranges from 1,100 to 1,250 metres above sea level. Their dream is to turn it into a 620-hectare winter recreation paradise with snowboarding, tobogganing, snowshoeing, and back-country skiing.

17

Profiles

The heart of any community lies within its people, and the Sunshine Coast's heart is filled with talented and dedicated individuals. While the size restrictions of this book have prevented me from writing about all of the wonderful musicians, writers, artists, craftspeople, sportspeople, and entrepreneurs who live here, those I have chosen to profile in the following pages epitomize the attitudes and activities of the Sunshine Coast lifestyle. I am indebted to each of the following for their hospitality and openness, and the privilege they accorded me by sharing their stories.

Matthew Baker, Native Carver

Michelle Bruce, Violinist and Conductor of Coast String Fiddlers

Candice Campo, Native interpretive guide–kayak trips

Dan Crosby, Marine support for film industry

Doug Detwiller, Mountain biker and creator of Sprockids

Reg and Lynne Dickson, Music makers

Stan Dixon, Politician and publisher of *KAHTOU*

Patricia Leigh Forst, Artist and vocalist

Judy Gill, Best-selling romance novelist

Lance & Monika Grey, Wholesale evergreens distributors

Conchita Harding, Dressmaker and film industry liaison

Sargeant Ed Hill, Artist and participator in RCMP Vision Quest tribal journey

Patricia Richardson Logie, Portrait Artist

Mary Covernton O'Brian, Roberts Creek pioneer

Barby Paulus, Weaver

Cindy Rudolph, Wildlife artist

John Seabrook, Knife maker

Randie Tame, Back-to-the-lander herb farmer

Lee Taylor and Leigh Blakey, Kitemakers

Howard and Mary White, Publishers

Violet Winegarden, Pioneer and founder of Happy Cat Haven

Matthew Baker

In the bungalow he shares with his wife Tina and their three small children, Matthew Baker puts the finishing touches on a yellow cedar plaque of a sea otter. The carving is ornamented with black and red geometric designs.

A tall man with an athletic build, he speaks so softly my recorder almost fails to pick up his voice. He was born in North Vancouver, he says, and grew up on the Squamish

Mathew Baker working on an otter carving.

Indian Reserve at Capilano. His mother, Marie Baker (née Jeffries) was from Sechelt; his father Richard Baker was a longshoreman and totem pole carver from Capilano. "As a boy I played lots of sports. Started lacrosse when I was five years old." His first memory of the Sunshine Coast was as a student at the Sechelt Residential School where he and his brothers were sent while his mother recovered from a stroke. The boys hated the school and ran away three times. "I missed my mom and dad."

When Matthew was small he would sneak his father's tools, escape to his room, and whittle on any wood he could find. "My great-grandfather lived with us when I was seven. He used to carve with my dad and great-uncles, and I just grew into it." By the age of thirteen he was helping his

father with the totem poles, some of which were sold to buyers in Germany and Japan. Later Matthew would sculpt six totems on his own for the Native House in Vancouver.

In the beginning he combined his artwork with jobs in carpentry and as a fisheries warden, and he had to travel a lot to sell his carvings. Eventually, however, he acquired an agent in Vancouver. "Now I don't have to worry about selling. My name's getting around, I guess. I do quality work."

Many of his sculptures incorporate native stories that were passed down to him from his grandmother, Katherine Jeffries (née Scow), who was a respected elder of the Sechelt Nation and the daughter of a Kwakwaka'wakw chief. Often, as with the sea otter he is working on, Matthew creates his own story using Kwakwaka'wakw designs.

With other pieces, he might follow a traditional legend. If the story belongs to his own family, he often includes it with the carving. Inspiration for his designs also comes from potlatches. As he carefully trims the shape of the otter's eye, he tells how his great-grandfather Sam Scow, who was a chief in Alert Bay, went to jail for 30 days for holding a potlatch. "Today," he adds, "anybody can hold a potlatch."

Mask and rattle making, he explains, revolve around native mask dancers. A few years ago a friend, whose grandfather was holding a potlatch in Bella Coola, asked him to make a sea otter mask with a mouth that would open and close. It was subsequently used in one of the ceremonial dances.

Obtaining most of his wood from abandoned logging slashes, Matthew searches carefully for material that is solid and dry, with no rot or termites. For wall plaques he generally uses yellow cedar because it leaves a nice finish, while red cedar is his choice for masks and totem poles. He starts a pole with a design he sees in his head, draws it on paper, then makes a model, scaling it to a log. Often he'll carve for twelve hours a day, and has developed a painful tendonitis that he casually shrugs off as just another part of life.

Whenever he wants a respite from wood, Mathew turns to making gold and silver jewellery, which he says is "easier to carve, as long as you have a steady hand." His metal designs are similar to those he does in wood, only smaller, with figures sometimes placed in different positions.

Although he never thought he'd want to live on the Sunshine Coast because of his residential school experience, after an extended visit with his Grandmother Jeffries five years ago, Matthew decided to move here permanently because "it's real quiet and slow."

When his grandmother died suddenly in 1999, he was deeply shaken. "I should have talked to her more," he says. Her funeral, held at Alert Bay, was attended by Chief Gary Feschuk and the Sechelt elders. "My aunt and cousins from Alert Bay said thank-you to the Sechelt Nation for their understanding about Granny going back home."

Matthew has most of the design figured out for a memorial pole he and his brother have promised to carve for her grave. When he finds a red cedar large enough to hold it, he'll put his heart and soul into cutting the story out of the wood just as his father and his grandfather and his great-grandfather did before him.

Michelle Bruce

The audience is unable to keep still as the lively notes of The Coast String Fiddlers fills the room. On stage the youngsters' expressions are serious as they concentrate on the music. Their conductor, Michelle Bruce, is a small woman with a lively face who clearly loves what she is doing. As her toe taps the floor in time with the beat, she leads the children through a medley of tunes while the audience claps along.

"Fiddling is my passion," says Michelle. "It's music you play more from the soul. It's happy music that makes people want to stomp their feet and get up and dance."

The eldest daughter of Vancouver folk singers, Don and Doreen Savien, Michelle was introduced to the violin when she was eight years old, taking lessons from Kenneth Yunke. At twelve she was playing in the Vancouver Philharmonic Youth Orchestra.

During the summer her family often stayed at an aunt's beachside cabin in Roberts Creek and it was here in 1966 that she met Chuck Bruce. They fell in love and ran away to a commune at French Bar Creek. Two years later they were married and moved to Roberts Creek where their son was born, and then their daughter. Caring for the children took up most of Michelle's time until 1980 when she got a job as a Special Education Teaching Assistant (SETA) with the school board where she worked for the next ten years.

Michelle Bruce with student Jane Estey at her Roberts Creek studio.

One day in the late 1980s Katie Engermeyer, a Sechelt physiotherapist and Suzuki violin teacher, invited Michelle to train in the Suzuki method and teach some of her students. "I thought she'd give me the little guys," Michelle says, "but she wanted me to take the advanced kids." Eventually Katie retired from teaching, leaving all of her students to Michelle.

By 1992 seven of the students were doing so well that Michelle wanted to give them an opportunity to play together. She approached Tom Kershaw, a retired doctor from Ontario who had studied conducting in Thunder Bay, and they started the

Sunshine Coast Community Orchestra. Now every Saturday morning she goes to the Roberts Creek School to conduct the youth orchestra. "It's just beautiful," she says. "All that sound coming to you. I can see why conductors have the longest life spans."

She's equally enthusiastic about how the other music teachers on the coast are encouraging their kids to participate in the orchestra. "It's such a good discipline—to play with others, to go their speed, and get this big sound that you don't get practising by yourself."

For the students who didn't want to join the orchestra, Michelle started a Friday night fiddle club, originally meeting in her basement. The late Ernie Chartrand, a cousin of the great Canadian fiddler Andy Desjarles, would come to the house and play along with the kids. "He wanted to play the slow stuff, and the kids wanted to play the fast stuff," Michelle remembers. "We have a fiddle award in his name at the Music Festival." Eventually the informal club became The Coast String Fiddlers.

In 1998 Michelle and principal Ann Skelcher began making plans to take the young fiddlers to the Joamie School in Iqaluit, and to have the Joamie fiddlers make a return visit to the Sunshine Coast. The fiddlers gave concerts almost every weekend to raise the $36,000 they would need to fly the eighteen youths (from age nine to eighteen) and four adults to Iqaluit. As the spring 2000 deadline approached the kids were still far from their goal. Then an anonymous donor contributed $5,000, which spurred others in the community to open their purses. "People just kept coming, and at every performance five hundred to six hundred dollars was going into the hat," Michelle says. "So we got there."

Besides the Youth Orchestra and the Coast String Fiddlers, Michelle teaches two other fiddle classes, the Horsetails and the Rosen Rasers. In her spare time she is concertmaster of the Symphony Orchestra and conducts the Intermediate Orchestra.

Michelle's mother also teaches Suzuki violin and plays with Michelle in a string quartet, Jane, Do, Mick & Mo. "Mom really encourages me. She is one of my major influences—the way she keeps going and introducing me to new music and new groups."

With Chuck ready for retirement, Michelle plans to cut back on some of her activities with the orchestras. It will give her more time to jam with her mom and to practise her own fiddling. "My goal" she says, "is to be able to fiddle as fast as those kids can!"

Candice Campo (X̱ets'emitsà)

As she paddles her teal-blue kayak towards Poise Island in Porpoise Bay, Candice Campo looks around for the seal that has taken to following her whenever she is on the inlet. His dark head pokes from the surface in her wake and she smiles her welcome, then returns to paddling, giving herself over to the tranquillity of the water. fter a while she pauses to rest. The kayak slows, but the seal, lost in its own world, keeps swimming, bumping into the kayak with a soft thud. "I don't know who was more startled, myself or the seal," she says.

In 1999 after taking kayak lessons from Karen Renfrew and Lynn Buckman of Porpoise Bay Kayak, Candice discovered not only a love for the sport, but an opportunity to share her knowledge of native lore and meet new people at the same time. Partnering with her two instructors, she guides kayakers to traditional Sechelt sites and shares the oral history of that area. Often the trips include visits to pictographs—the ancient rock paintings that can be found along the shores of Sunshine Coast inlets. "One of our most sacred areas is at Chatterbox Falls," she says. "That's where our people say the Creator rested after he made the land and the animals and the Shishalh people." After a lunch break—a meal of smoke salmon, salads, beverages and dessert provided by the tour company—there is more

Candice Campo

story telling and sometimes lessons in drumming. If there is time she teaches the bone game. "It's a really fun game that everybody is welcome to participate in."

Named X̱ets'emitsà after her grandmother Sarah Jane Baptiste (née Jefferies), Candice is the daughter of Rose and Wayne Clark. Although very close to her father, it was her mother and stepfather Vincent Paul who raised her to be, as she puts it, "connected to the land." She remembers gathering clams from the Porpoise Bay mudflats in the days before they became polluted, and going to the government wharf to fish for salmon or jig for herring.

The era of the residential school had ended by the time Candice started kindergarten, but as the native and non-native children in Sechelt came together at the elementary school, race relations were, she says quietly, "still in great need of improvement." She pauses then adds, "There were some unfortunate experiences. But I just have to look at the way it is today and be grateful for my daughter that she gets to grow up in a more open and friendly community."

From a very young age Candice became interested in the history of her people, listening to the stories told by her elders. One of her first summer jobs as a teenager was to welcome visitors to the band's salmon enhancement hatchery, sharing its history and details of the projects they were working on. Since earning her degree at Simon Fraser University in 1977 she has worked with the band on research projects including an animal species identification project, a three-year traditional use study, and an ongoing oral history project. She has also become a well-known storyteller and often visits local schools to share native history with children.

Eventually Candice plans to offer her own tours through Talaysay Tourism, a business she has named after her daughter. Her goal is to share her expertise with fellow band members who she believes "have a wealth of information through their own family history and backgrounds that would make them excellent tour guides." For now, however, she's concentrating on learning how to run a business, occasionally slipping away to her kayak and a quiet place on the water where she can lay back, close her eyes and listen to the shore birds, the ducks, and the soft splash of rising fish.

Dan Crosby

Dan Crosby is an ordinary kind of a guy: medium height, clean shaven, mild mannered. Born at Ocean Falls in 1952, he moved with his parents to Gibsons two years later. Dan loved the water and by the age of fourteen he was already fishing on commercial boats. When he was fifteen he left home, and at seventeen he was beachcombing for logs along the Sunshine Coast. During slack periods he went back to fishing or to towing and booming logs.

In 1973 CBC began filming the television series *The Beachcombers* in Gibsons, and like a lot of young people on the coast, Dan suddenly found himself involved in the film industry when he and his friends were hired to provide background boats. "I know so many people who got their start in the film business because of that series," he says.

Because of his expertise on the water, Dan became involved in stunt work with fellow beachcomber, John Smith. Occasionally doubling for Bruno Gerussi, Dan did everything from running boats across log booms to having his craft blown up. "Inside the boat they have these things like a big wok filled with gasoline and stuff to make the special effects explosion. You have to wear fire retardant suits and be gelled up." Although it looks frightening, he maintains that the special effects crew always put safety first.

Dan Crosby

Before *The Beachcombers* ended their nineteen-year run, Dan was already at work with another series called *Danger Bay* filmed in Indian Arm and East Howe Sound. Since only three or four episodes might be related to water, income from the film work wasn't constant and he continued to log and beachcomb, often in the rugged waters off the west coast of Vancouver Island.

Today his company, Crosby Marine Services Ltd., still hauls logs and equipment for the logging industry, but they are also the top marine support service for the film industry in Vancouver. "Anything they need on the water, we supply them." He and his crew travel to wherever they are needed, from the west coast of Vancouver Island to the Queen Charlotte Islands. Often this requires working 20 to 45 hours at a stretch, as when the boats were needed for a shoot at Britannia Beach one day and at Steveston the next.

The company's permanent staff of five can swell to as high as 28 employees for a feature film, and while some of the specialists, such as certified divers, come from Vancouver, most of the crew are hired out of Gibsons. It is here, too, that Dan makes his home on a hill overlooking the harbour. "I can't imagine being in another place in B.C.," he says. Unfortunately most filming is done in Vancouver and consequently Dan has had to spend a lot of time away from his family.

When he's in Gibsons, Dan often volunteers his services for events held at the wharf. Canoe racers use his barge to get on and off the dock, and in June 1999 during the Maritime Weekend, visitors were able to walk down off the dock and onto his barge to view 25 visiting tugboats. The International Retired Tugboat Association was so impressed with the system and the reception from the Town of Gibsons that they plan to return.

In 2000 Dan's company provided marine support for the Hallmark Entertainment feature film, *Voyage of the Unicorn*. That summer Dan persuaded the producers to lend him the *Unicorn* and troll boat for a skit to be performed at the Gibsons Sea Calvalcade. With the help of production costumes and the film's special effects team, a sea battle was waged in the harbour, with the evil trolls kidnapping Mayor Barry Janyk from the *Unicorn*. The battle ended when the trolls shot a background boat that had been loaded with explosives, the resulting fireworks thrilling spectators gathered on the wharf and breakwater.

Dan says that next year they won't have the *Unicorn* vessels, but he's sure they'll think of something just as spectacular. In the meantime, he's anticipating the day when he can turn the business over to his son and spend more time just sitting and looking out at the harbour from his living room window. As we watched a harvest moon rise above the mountains and shimmer down on the water, it was easy to appreciate his latest goal.

Doug Detwiller

The walls of Doug Detwiller's classroom are covered with action posters and the cupboards overflowing with training gear. Parked beneath the blackboard is a row of mountain bikes. "If I'm teaching ratios I'll use the gears of the bike to show how ratios work," he explains. "Then we'll go for a ride and the students realize it's an important thing to know." The bikes are also part of an international program he has developed called "Sprockids" that helps young people build self-esteem and develop anger management skills while they're learning to mountain bike.

Doug's love for the outdoors began during his childhood summers spent roaming the beaches and trekking through the woods around his grandparents' summer home on Gower Point. After graduating from teacher training in 1979 he accepted a position at Cedar Grove Elementary and moved to the Sunshine Coast. His interest in mountain biking began in 1990 when he bought a couple of beater bikes in the *Buy & Sell.* A few months later he entered the Brody Test of Metal race in Roberts Creek. He was 35 then, and although he looks like a

Doug Detwiller in his Gibsons Elementary classroom.

big kid in t-shirt and denims, he was intimidated by the thought of competing with a much younger generation. "I thought they would be sort of negative about an older person trying to ride. Instead they were just incredibly positive. Their camaraderie, energy, and friendship made the whole stigma of different generations totally disappear. I think that's what really hooked me on it."

He was so hooked that when the fall term began he went into a school assembly at Gibsons Elementary where he was teaching and asked if anyone was interested in a mountain bike club. Two hundred students showed up at the first meeting and Sprockids was born. He wrote an instruction manual, got other teachers involved, and developed a series of races designed more for fun than competition. "The program just started to grow and take on a life of its own. I kept finding more and more ways to use it working with kids."

When his elementary students graduated to high school and asked, "Now what?" he formed a club outside of the elementary school. With permission from the Regional District, the Town of Gibsons, and the Ministry of Forests, club members started building the Sprockids Mountain Bike Park at the old Gibsons landfill site, learning about the environment and trail building while still taking care of the land.

"I started the project as a way of getting kids involved and feeling good about themselves," Doug explains. The students help themselves and each other through caring for their bikes and the trails. The older kids act as group leaders and mentors to younger riders. "There are a ton of great kids building trails and maintaining them," he says proudly. "They're out on their holidays cleaning up garbage, and the community has seen it." As a result Sprockids has received tremendous local support. "It's teaching kids the skills and values to make it in the world. Like it's okay to make mistakes. Goal setting. Challenging yourself. All these things in a non-stressful environment."

The trails are "user friendly" and have become increasingly popular, especially after they were featured in a 1999 Kokanee Ride Guide on the cable television station ESPN's Outdoor Life Network. "We have incredible scenery," Doug says. "The woods from Elphinstone all the way up to Pender Harbour are honeycombed with old logging roads and trails. We can offer mountain biking at any level, from beginners to intermediate to expert riding." The trails also provide a lesson in local history. "We found log cabins and the old flume where they used to skid down cedar blocks from way up the mountain."

Many of Doug's evenings are spent helping kids rebuild bikes. He believes there's something almost zen-like in constructing a bike from just a frame, creating a vehicle that allows everything from a quiet little ride to a speedy, adrenalin kick.

In 1997 a group that included world-class racers Alison Sydor, Lesley Tomlinson, and Bruce Spicer formed the Sprockids Program Development Society, a non-profit organization that promotes and develops the program. Now implemented in five countries, it has become so popular that Race Face, a company specializing in mountain bike equipment and clothing, bought one day per week of Doug's teaching time to enable him to revise his 200-page manual for its third printing. *Sprockids: The Two-Wheeled Approach to Building Self-Esteem* covers everything from riding skills, organizing races and using mountain biking in the school curriculum, to video skills, mechanics, and accessories. The most recent edition includes a road safety program and a ten-week lesson plan.

Although he is overwhelmed by the success of his project, the real triumph for Doug is the magic he still experiences biking with the kids. "I'm riding up on top of the mountain with some of my grade twelves. As I pant up, these boys are sitting around saying, 'God, I love it up here—so beautiful and quiet.' I thought they'd be talking about the new girl in school or whatever. Instead they're discovering life and nature and all those things."

Lynne and Reg Dickson

As Lynne Dickson dances around her studio, nine waltzing five-year-olds vie for a spot next to her. Later, sitting cross-legged on a carpet, they happily sing "The Bear Went Over the Mountain," waving teddy bears in time with the beat. Although a grandmother, this short, brown-haired lady looks much like the children she's teaching as she croons softly to the teddy she holds.

Lynne and Reg Dickson at Lynne's studio in Wilson Creek.

Reg Dickson, who teaches the Guitar Gang—mostly boys—of older students, shares her youthful enthusiasm, possibly because music is something they both grew up with. Lynne studied piano and dance as a child in Burnaby. In Ontario Reg listened to his parents on guitar and accordion and participated in family sing-alongs. When he was sixteen he purchased his own guitar and taught himself how to play.

In 1972 Reg and Lynne moved to the Sunshine Coast. In his spare time he played gigs and studied classical guitar, and when their three children were all old enough for school, she got a job as playground aide at their Davis Bay School where she soon started a small choir.

One evening in the late 1980s Lynne and Reg attended a school staff party and started jamming with Michelle Bruce. It was so much fun that the three decided to write an album and in 1989 published *Christmas With Harmony*. Unfortunately, just after the album came out, one of the Dickson's daughters was seriously injured in a car accident and required treatment off the coast. It wasn't until the day before Christmas that their daughter recovered enough for the whole family to return home. "That's when we came to really feel that this community was special,"

Lynne says. "Our house was clean and decorated, there was baking here, and people we didn't even know were coming to our door and giving us money and baking ... it was absolutely amazing!"

After deciding that teaching music was what she really wanted to do, Lynne went to UBC and studied Carl Orff's method of training. For a while she worked with the Westwind School of Music in Davis Bay, and when it closed down she got a grant from Community Futures to start her own school. Using games, rhythmic exercises, and folk music in what she describes as "a combination of the Orff method, Kodaly, and Dalcroze Eurythmics," she developed her own unique way of teaching that she took to local day-care centres and schools. In 2000 she moved into a studio at Davis Bay and students began coming to her. "It's really great," she says happily. "I had two hundred and thirty students a week this year."

Besides instructing adults and older children, Lynne has a Baby Fun class where children as young as twelve months—with the help of their parents—sing, march, and do rhythmic exercises. "Some of the parents have been too frightened to sing their whole lives," Lynne says. "Then they come here, and although it's only nursery rhymes, they're feeling so good that they actually start singing to their children at home."

By the time the children reach the age of three they come to a class without their parents. At age six they can participate in the children's division of Lynne's two Music Makers choirs, and take part in an annual concert at Rockwood Lodge. "It's amazing," she marvels, "how many tiny, tiny children can sing on pitch."

Besides his Guitar Gang, Reg leads the men's section of the Music Makers adult choir. For the past five years the Dicksons, Michelle Bruce, and Kathleen Hovey have put on a four-week Music Makers' Summer Camp for kids. With a program of musical theatre, chamber music, fiddling, and guitar, the camp became so popular that attendance swelled from 40 kids to 160. "Next year we'll break into three separate camps," Lynne says. "Michelle will do a Fiddling Camp, Kathleen a Chamber Camp, and we'll do a Musical Theatre Camp."

Since *Christmas With Harmony*, Reg and Lynne have cut two more successful CDs: *Light the Lights* and *Walk in the Wind*. Profits from their sales have been donated to groups like Breakaway, Rockwood Lodge, and Cystic Fibrosis of Canada. In 1999 the couple were awarded the Sechelt Chamber of Commerce's Good Citizen of the Year Award for the positive and enthusiastic contribution they've made to Sechelt with their music.

Stan Dixon

Stan Dixon personifies the positive relationship that has evolved between the native and non-native communities of the Sunshine coast, and the transition his people have made from being wards of the federal Indian Act to becoming self-governed. He has been elected to the band, regional, and municipal governments, hosted local radio and television programs, and developed a native newspaper with a national readership. In his spare time he's off to other parts of the country on speaking engagements, or to represent British Columbia at the National Association of Friendship Centres.

Stan Dixon on the beach in front of his Kahtou *newspaper office.*

The son of a logger and a cannery worker, Theodore and Mary Joe Goldie, Stan and his oldest brother Ted spent their childhood with their mother's parents, Captain Joe and Sophie Dixon, at their Deserted Bay home. They both attended residential school in Sechelt until grade eight when they were transferred to St. Mary's Residential School in Mission, and finally to the integrated St. Thomas Acquinas Catholic High School in North Vancouver from which they graduated in 1960.

The greatest influence on his life, he maintains, was his grandfather, who was born in 1872 when the Indian Act was not yet in full force. "He told us … you must be the best, take care of yourselves, and become independent. Then you'll be happy

and free." Captain Joe was always helping others. Says Stan, "I knew early on that he loved us, he cared for us and his people."

At the age of fourteen Stan was spending his summers setting chokers for a logging contractor at Earls Cove. In 1961 he took a job as a longshoreman on the Port Mellon docks with brothers Ted and Russell, but after three years he returned to logging, and eventually established Kwatamus Trucking Incorporated. He entered the political arena in 1972 by winning a seat on the Sechelt Indian Band council, where Chief Henry Paul encouraged him to read about native politics. A year later he was also hired to do maintenance work at the residential school, where Father

Fitzgerald taught him how the federal political process worked and how to influence federal bureaucrats. The priest also urged him to be patient because change takes time.

Two years after Ted's death in an auto accident in 1981, Stan was elected chief. In this position he was instrumental in helping the Sechelt Indian Band (SIB) achieve self-government. "Our negotiating team wanted freedom, so we never talked about aboriginal title or aboriginal rights or sovereignty in our public discussions or with any government representatives ... and it brought results. It gave us ownership of our reserve lands." Bill C-93, *The Sechelt Indian Band's Self-Government Act*, was proclaimed on October 9, 1986. "We brought the documents home in my brother Ted's briefcase," he says. "Bill C-93 set us free."

But the battle wasn't over. There were more negotiations with the provincial government so that the lessees would have representation on the Sechelt Band land, and in 2004 the resulting "sunset clause" will have to be reviewed and ratified. It was also necessary for the attitudes of his people to change from what Stan calls "the Indian Act mentality," where they looked to the government to direct their lives. "We had to fight to free ourselves from the welfare state. We did it ... and today I'm still proud of our self-government achievement. Fortunately for our Shishalh people,

we are slowly moving in the right direction—to self-reliance. There is a light at the end of the tunnel."

Although Stan lost the 1987 SIB council election, he won the position of Area C director of the Sunshine Coast Regional District later that year. After serving as Parks Chairman until 1990, he went on to win a seat on the Sechelt municipal council. In both of these positions he feels he has been able to develop a greater understanding between the native and non-native communities. "Both sides," he says, "need to respect and understand each other. People need to co-operate and share to enhance a sustainable and healthy community." Since 1993 he has also been involved provincially and nationally in the Aboriginal Friendship Centre Society, which advocates on behalf of the aboriginal people in urban areas.

In 1991 Stan purchased *KAHTOU*, a monthly native newspaper that he runs with his wife Lori and sister-in-law Lee from his office building on the Trail Bay waterfront. Downstairs is the fitness centre that he opened in 1982. "The first aboriginal-owned business on SIB land," he says proudly.

It would not be surprising to see Stan running for a provincial or federal position, but for now he's content with Sunshine Coast politics, working to "reduce racism by bringing our people to understanding, respect, and self determination."

Patricia Leigh Forst

In her wall murals Patricia "Pat" Forst can capture the warmth of a sunset or the grace of a heron. The burnt umber stain she uses, fired at just the right temperature, gives a wonderful bronze quality to her pieces, and the soft contours of rocks and figures glow with life.

"I'm very influenced by the scenery around us," she says. "I really love the water and the islands and the trees ... and I prefer simplicity."

Beside her backyard goldfish pond is a unique fountain where water trickles past a combination of rocks and small Mayan-like sculptures, down through a series of fluted red-earth-coloured bowls, and into the pond. Simple, yet like her other sculptures, ever-changing as the light and shadows shift.

In her studio gallery copper-looking sunfish swim above elegant vases that rest on driftwood posts. On shelves are other pieces of pottery—teapots, bowls, and plates—of traditional and original designs that she and other local potters have created. For some of her own works Pat has used a process called slips and scrafitto in which a slurry of coloured clay is applied to a pot, hardened, then cut with a tool, simultaneously producing colour and decoration.

The daughter of a naval officer and a music teacher, Patricia spent much of her childhood travelling between Ontario and Victoria. She studied pottery and sculpture at Emily Carr School of Art, the Vancouver Art School, and Capilano College, and earned a degree in Recreation Education at UBC. After graduation she and her husband William "Bill" and their baby son lived on Hornby Island for a year until Bill found a teaching position on the Sunshine Coast.

Patricia Leigh Forst at her studio in Gibsons.

Patricia continued to study pottery in between looking after their two sons, taking singing lessons, and working at various jobs, including a trail-building project at Soames Hill Park near her home, and a year as the manager of the Arts Centre in Sechelt. One of her teachers was Robin Hopper, an internationally acclaimed potter and author who specialized in glaze development. To create his designs he employs the Golden Mean—a Greek equation that is used to calculate the ratio of the body to its parts. "I used it to design some of my own pots," says Pat, "and boy they would walk out the door!"

In 1987, when their boys were thirteen and sixteen, the Forsts went to England where Bill was filling an exchange teaching position. While he taught and the boys attended school, Patricia would go into London and visit art galleries and museums. "I went to England thinking I would look at pots, and I ended up looking at sculpture," she says. "It was sort of a message to me to change directions." She attended a community college and took courses in painting and drawing, and one in pottery, and started doing wall murals. On her return to the Sunshine Coast she had a successful exhibition of the murals at the Arts Centre.

When she starts working on a mural, Patricia seldom knows how the sculpture will turn out. "I lay out the clay so it's all squished together as I go around and I build it up and eventually it goes one way or another. When the clay is harder, I use a tool—kind of like a grater—and smooth it, so you can never tell the sculpture is made out of coils."

Pottery is labour intensive and expensive to produce: it costs two hundred dollars just to fire up the kiln. Selling from her own gallery reduces costs, but Pat still displays a few pieces at the Gibsons Landing Gallery and Jack's Bistro. Her wall murals are marketed in Vancouver on a commission basis through the Van Dop Gallery and Kate Holland Landscaping. She also runs a weekend drop-in program and teaches pottery in the workshop at the back of the gallery, running a one-week course through Capilano College in Sechelt where she works two days a week as a continuing education co-ordinator.

Rivalling Patricia's passion for pottery is her love of music. As a girl she took lessons from her mother and later studied for ten years with Lyn Vernon. "Three years ago I actually ended up winning the highest award at the local music festival," she says, sounding amazed. A soprano soloist, she sings with the Reflections choir. Her family has also participated in many of the Music Society's productions. "I was the publicity person for the Music Society," she says. "We did *Pirates of Penzance* one year so I made pirate flags for everybody's car."

Judy Gill

Forty shiny paperbacks, each with its own romantic character pictured on the cover, fill a shelf above Judy Gill's computer desk. She's written them all. A descendent of early Pender Harbour pioneers, Robert L. and Eileen Vaughan Griffith, Judy grew up in Egmont with four siblings and countless cousins. "We played wonderful games of imagination," she remembers. "A lot of them based on stories we had read." Her best friend was the Open Shelf Library in Victoria, which sent a "library van" to small communities such as Egmont.

At the newly built high school at Kleindale she met English teacher, Frances L. Fleming, who inspired her to write. "She gave me wings. She recognized that I had talent and encouraged me so much!" It was here, too, that Judy got her first taste of publishing as editor of the school newspaper and annual.

After graduation and journalism courses at a Vancouver night school she joined the army and trained as a nurse. Inevitably, she fell in love with a soldier, Robert "Bob" Gill. "There were forty women to two thousand men," she says wryly. "Not very good odds for a woman who had decided she wanted to stay single forever." On her web page, however, she pronounces her marriage of 37 years a success: "I wanted someone who would love me with the same dedication my father showed my mother

Romance novelist, Judy Gill.

and who would expect an equal degree of love and fealty in return. I found it."

It was while the couple was stationed in Germany that a friend saw her trading romance books with his wife and remarked, "You two read so much of that, why don't you write one?" Unable to resist a challenge, Judy started writing. Her youngest daughter was in kindergarten and she had three hours each day to herself. She sold the first book she wrote, *Name Me This Feeling*, to Women's Weekly Library in 1975. "I got what amounted to eight hundred dollars and immediately went out and bought myself something I wanted without looking at the price tag—a green terrycloth bathing suit cover. If it had cost the whole eight hundred dollars I think I'd still have bought it."

Although Judy wrote and published six books while in Germany, when she and Bob moved to the Sunshine Coast in 1979, her energies went into building their home and working full time at a local bookstore. It wasn't until 1987 that she returned to writing novels, and *Head Over Heels* became the first of 24 books that she would write for Bantam Books in New York. She has also written for Robinson Scarlet, Harlequin Love and Laughter, Doubleday, and Robert Hale, Ltd. Recently her first electronic book, *Seekers of the Dawn*, was published by New Concepts Publishing.

Looking at the books above her desk, Judy smiles. "Now I get between two thousand and twelve thousand dollars U.S. in advances against royalties, as well as residual royalties and foreign sales." She has won awards of excellence and some of her books have made the top ten on U.S. bestseller lists. Her latest dream is to sell a script for one of her humour novels to Disney for a movie.

Writing is a joy for Judy and the best times are when she and Bob and her laptop computer go out in their boat and anchor in a quiet spot where she can write, undisturbed by telephones and neighbourhood noises. She begins a story by describing a scene. "I'm a very visual writer," she explains. "I see the characters doing something and it just seems to flow from there. Often I've written a hundred pages of manuscript before I really know who they are and why they're doing what they're doing."

She believes very strongly in the importance of family. "I don't just write about a man-woman relationship. I also write about her relationships with friends and children and family, and how they combine to create a woman who is a whole being."

Today she and Bob live in a Sechelt condo in the same complex as her mother. Their eldest daughter Shannon has a home in Halfmoon Bay with her husband and two children, and their youngest daughter Tara resides on Galiano Island. "My roots are here," Judy says. "I couldn't conceive of being anywhere else. This is where I need to be."

Lance and Monika Grey

From mid-September until the second week in December the yard and workrooms of Selma Park Evergreens smells like Christmas. Mounds of evergreen boughs fill every free space, waiting to be packed and shipped to markets from Vancouver to Nova Scotia, where they are used for everything from simple floral displays to decorations for Christmas banquets. By the second week in December the yards are bare, and salal, huckleberry, boxwood, and tiger fern have replaced the evergreens in the workroom and trailers.

Owned by Lance and Monika Grey, the business was originally started in 1970 by Monika's parents Don and Monty Shinn at their home on Selma Park Road. Don had picked brush in the northwestern United States prior to immigrating to Canada. He started Selma Park Evergreens by picking and purchasing salal and cedar, bundling and packing it in their backyard. Monty helped by delivering the brush to Vancouver. In 1980 Don bought out Reid Fern & Moss and began shipping his products back east. Needing more space, he moved his plant to Inlet Avenue near Porpoise Bay.

When she graduated from high school, Monika joined the team as a bookkeeper. Eight years ago she and Lance bought the business, which now has three full-time and seven part-time employees, and purchases salal and other brush from over 50

Evergreens are piled in every available corner at Selma Park Evergreens, ready to be shipped to markets across Canada.

regular pickers on the Sunshine Coast and many others off the coast.

"Our product comes from all over the province," says Lance. "The boxwood comes out of the Salmon Arm area, white pine from Nakusp, and Ponderosa pine from Merritt."

Their fleet of five trucks enables them to pick up the evergreens at distant locations and bring them to their Porpoise Bay plant where they are graded, cased, refrigerated, and finally shipped to buyers. "Keeps BC Ferries in business," Lance remarks humorously, then explains that it makes economic sense to use Sechelt as their home base. "Salal is our main product throughout the year, and the majority of it comes from here or Powell River."

During their busiest season up to six truckloads a week are shipped out. "That's 850 cases per truck, and each case weights 50 pounds," says Lance who works seven fifteen-hour days a week for the three months prior to Christmas.

Most of their orders are received by phone or fax and although the couple rarely meet their buyers in person they have a steady clientele. It's difficult, however, for the Greys to take on new customers because they don't have enough pickers to meet the demand even though, Lance maintains, the majority make a good living. "They support a family and make mortgage payments like any other person," he says. Others are happy if they make twenty dollars a week, and some go out just for the exercise.

Most pickers have their own vehicle, but a few walk out to their salal patch each morning, pick all day, then walk home and phone Lance to tell him where he can collect their bundles. "They're making the best of what they have," he says.

Besides providing many local residents with employment, the Greys believe their business makes a unique contribution to the local economy. "The money that we bring here is from all over Canada," Lance explains. "Hundreds of thousands of dollars—to be spent on the Sunshine Coast." Their product is also a renewable resource as whatever is picked grows back in one season.

Conchita Harding

On February 19, 1974, Conchita Harding, an eighteen-year-old Mexican woman, stood in the forward lounge of the Langdale ferry. Only mildly aware of the grey, choppy sea or the rain slashing against the windows, she stared with a mixture of fright and awe at the snow-capped coastal mountains surrounding Howe Sound, and wondered, *Where is this place? How far do I have to go?*

Born in Guadalajara, Mexico, Conchita was used to sunshine and sandy beaches. A commerce graduate, she was also a qualified high school teacher and first year medical student. In 1972 she met David Harding, a Sunshine Coast fisherman who was vacationing in the village of San Patricio where Conchita was volunteering as an interpreter. Two years later they were married and on their way to live at his parent's home in Gibsons.

At first Conchita couldn't stop sending letters to her parents describing the beauty of the mountains and islands, but as the winter dragged into a cold, wet spring she began to worry. She asked David's mom, "Do you ever see the sunshine?"

By the time the sun did appear, David was away fishing, and Conchita was left in their newly purchased house to cope with loneliness and the challenge of adapting to a new culture. "I thought, okay this is my home, this is where my children are going to be

*Conchita Harding
at her home in Gibsons.*

raised. I have to make friends with other people. So I just went out and started talking to my neighbours."

Her vitality and cheerful nature were appealing and, she says, "I was very lucky. I was accepted in the community. We still have friends from that time and they feel like a second family."

When her sons were born, Conchita was content to stay at home and look after them. By the time they started school, however, she was ready to resume her career. Discovering that her Mexican teaching certificates were not recognized in Canada, she relied instead on training she'd taken in sewing and fashion design. "My mother took sewing lessons in Mexico," she says, "and I used to go after school and wait for her." While she had waited Conchita watched and learned and that fall she enrolled in the three-year sewing course.

In Gibsons, Conchita began designing clothes for larger women, mostly acquaintances who liked the outfits she'd sewn for herself. Soon her dressmaking became a successful business. Influenced somewhat by the work of Giorgio Armani, she gets many of the inspirations for her designs by studying people and imagining how she might add practicality and comfort to their outfits. "I look at a lady who has a blouse and the buttonholes are in the wrong area. I think of her needs and then I just pour my ideas into a piece of paper."

Although she designs all types of clothing, Conchita specializes in wedding and graduation gowns. To compete with the Vancouver manufacturers, she offers a personal service, getting to know each client and designing a gown to suit their personality and budget. Everything is steam-pressed and delivered whenever it's needed, and on the morning of the wedding she is there to make sure everything is perfect for the bride.

Her fashion shows in Vancouver, Victoria, and on the Sunshine Coast are popular events. "The first time I did one in Sechelt we hit the front page with my design." At one successful exhibit, held at the Hotel Vancouver, her audience included members of the royal family from Norway.

An active volunteer in her children's schools, Conchita also joined the Gibsons Chamber of Commerce. As president in 1993–94, she implemented programs such as the Christmas Cash Campaign with the Sunshine Coast Credit Union, which provides interest-free loans for up to six months for residents who do their Christmas shopping on the coast. She now represents the Sunshine Coast on the advisory board of BC Ferries, and sits on the advisory board of Capilano College. On the side she has contributed her time and talents to the Lion's Club and the Maritime Museum and was instrumental in organizing the artists co-op in Gibsons. Lately she has been promoting the town of Gibsons to the film industry.

In 1992 Conchita obtained her Canadian citizenship. Standing beside the flags of her native and adoptive countries, she watched the Mexican flag slowly being lowered. "That was my home," she recalls nostalgically. "Where I was born and where I was brought up. My family is there." Then she smiles. "But it wasn't sad because I really belong here now."

Ed Hill

Ed Hill is one of those people who are born to challenge their world and he's willing to try just about anything that sparks his interest. His self-professed addictive personality drives him to seek perfection, and he believes passionately that health, family, and friends should be the priorities in a person's life. You can find him at most Sunshine Coast events—he's the proud officer dressed in red serge at formal ceremonies, the friendly guy wearing casual clothes and a baseball cap at community festivals, the concerned citizen speaking frankly to a crowd of parents about family values, the painter lost in concentration as he tries to capture the feeling of an inlet sunset.

Born in Paris, Ontario in 1948, Ed spent most of his youth in Peterborough. In high school he developed a love of drawing while taking commercial art lessons and even applied to an art college. His hatred of the growing drug culture, however, and what it was doing to his friends caused him in 1968 to put aside his dream of an art career and join the RCMP where he worked for many years as an undercover officer with the drug squad.

In 1979 Ed, his wife Joy, and their two children moved to Bella Bella where he had two-year posting as head of that detachment. By the time they left Ed had made such deep friendships within the First Nations

Sargeant Ed Hill with his Vision Quest memorabilia. Top right painting is Sheep Standing By Himself, *a collaboration between Ed Hill and Roy Henry Vickers.*

community that he was adopted by a native family and given a tribal name.

When he was transferred to Tofino in 1984 Ed became friends with artist, Roy Henry Vickers. One day he decided to play a trick on Roy by painting a scene, copying the artist's style. He planned to frame the picture and hang it in Roy's gallery, then watch his reaction. Before the project was complete, however, Roy walked in. He picked up the painting, studied it a moment, and then tore it in two. "If you're going to paint in my style, then you're going to do it right," he said sternly. Collecting the proper paint, brushes, and paper from his gallery, he returned to Hill's house and began giving him lessons.

"He took me through the whole process and I did a painting called *Old Man*. It's a silhouette of an old blue heron on a piling with its shoulders hunched against the sea, fog coming in." It was a simple piece, done predominantly in greys, and when it was finished Ed hung it on his wall, thinking that was the end of the exercise. Roy had a different plan. He financed a limited edition print of the painting, taught Ed how to handle and care for the prints, then framed and hung them in his Tofino gallery. By the end of the year that edition had sold out and Ed Hill was hooked on painting.

Developing his own style, which he describes as his personal translation of serenity and colour through the use of well-defined, clean, sharp lines, Ed has produced 23 limited edition works, five of them collaborations with Roy, Lyall Nanson, and Greta Guzek. Such combinations, he believes, produce unique paintings "that would never have existed had you not worked together ... something that can never be done again unless those two artists do it."

One of these collaborations took place in 1995 when Roy Vickers began an organization called Vision Quest to build a recovery centre "for all addictions for all people." He contacted Ed Hill to work with him on a painting, the proceeds of which would go towards the centre. The result was *Sheep Standing by Himself.* "I don't think it's the best piece I've worked on," Ed observed, "but in terms of inspiration and power it was unbelievable ... I suppose I'm looking for that again in my art. I want to get knocked off my feet."

Ed and Roy also took part in the 1997 RCMP Vision Quest tribal journey. Paddling native war canoes designed by Roy, Quest participants travelled from Hazelton in the Gitxan First Nation's territory, to Prince Rupert where they joined the First Nations' Tribal Journey and continued on to Victoria. The whole experience, says Ed, was "extremely spiritual, intense and personal ... the emotion of gift giving and sharing, of mending, of healing between the native people and the white people, between the police and the native communities … it was draining at times."

That December Ed was transferred to head the Gibsons' RCMP detachment. In his spare time he wrote a 150,000-word manuscript about the Vision Quest adventure. It has been sealed in the Gibsons time capsule, buried in 1999, and he's submitted a condensed version for publication.

After his retirement Ed plans to remain on the Sunshine Coast. He likes the way the community enthusiastically supports events like the canoe races and local fairs and festivals, and how it rallies around folks who need help, whether it's funding the food bank, collecting donations for the victims of a house fire, or purchasing a special van for the family of a handicapped child. It fits with his vision of family and friends and, he says, "makes the Sunshine Coast a nice and relatively safe place to live."

Patricia Richardson Logie

Two sets of Dutch doors lead off the front porch of Patricia Logie's bungalow, one opening into a small studio, the other to the living space she shares with her husband, Robert. Their sitting room is fronted by a low deck and a view of Howe Sound and distant, purple hills. She designed the cottage herself and deliberately kept it small. "I don't want to spend my time cleaning," she says in her no-nonsense manner. "I want to paint."

Her studio walls are filled with portraits, images alive with character and emotion. Brushes stand on a worktable, bristles up, in containers that are surrounded by crinkled paint tubes. A chenille scarf in muted browns is draped over an antique screen behind an easy chair.

Settling into the chair she explains that understanding her subject's inner self and expressing that in the painting is more important to her than achieving a perfect likeness. "You have to decide what you're going to show in portraits. A likeness isn't enough for me. I have to have the inner person."

Although by the age of twelve she could draw all of her classmates, it wasn't until she was 45 that Patricia began painting seriously. Her two oldest children had left home and she and her husband and their fifteen-year-old twins went to England for a year. There she studied at the John Cass College in London. "When I

Patricia Richardson Logie

was coming home on the trains each afternoon I was constantly looking at people's noses and eyes and the turn of their heads. I just got so enthused!"

Her enthusiasm produced dramatic results, with exhibitions in England with The Cass Group, The Royal Society of Portrait Painters, The Society of Women Artists, and the Pastel Society, as well as a tenure at Harrods as "Artist-in-Residence." Back in Canada she exhibited with the Federation of Canadian Artists, and in several Vancouver and Calgary art galleries.

While teaching portraiture at the University of British Columbia in 1979, she happened to see a textbook used in the native education program that was filled with images of natives as impoverished street people. "I got so annoyed that they should look at themselves in such a negative way," she says angrily. "How were they ever going to become proud of themselves if all they saw were these woebegone people?" She decided that she would paint aboriginal people who were like those she had known throughout her life, people with dignity and pride, and who were making positive contributions to their communities. The result was *Chronicles of Pride*, a collection of portraits published by Detselig Enterprises Ltd. in 1990.

"I didn't realize the work I was undertaking," she writes in her forward to the second chapter, "the years of constant research, speaking, administrating, and eventually not having time to paint."

One of the most difficult parts of *Chronicles of Pride* was trying to find a native person to write the text to go with the pictures. When she was unable to make that connection, she wrote it herself. "The only mess-up was that those ten years of work ruined my handwriting. I was on the telephone making notes the whole time and my writing, which was quite lovely, turned into a scribble!"

When the book was finished, Patricia toured extensively, showing her paintings in schools, galleries, and museums. Since then *Chronicles of Pride* has been placed on the suggested list of school curricula, and a video and teacher's resource guide have been produced to accompany it into classrooms. In 1991 she received the Silver Eagle Feather Award from the Professional Native Women's Association for her contribution to the native community.

Her next goal is to find a permanent home for the portraits, currently stored in crates in her studio. "They should be shown," she says, "because they have such an impact. People become aware of the differences between us, and the things that aren't different between us."

A year after *Chronicles of Pride* was published, Patricia and her husband moved to Hopkins Landing and for a while she turned her attention to watercolours and ink. "But figurative work is my favourite," she says, "and I want to get back to it." A member of the Sunshine Coast Artists Co-op, she recently held an exhibition of her nudes in "A Celebration of Beauty" at the Silk Purse Gallery in West Vancouver.

Mary Covernton O'Brian

Mary Covernton was only three weeks old when she first visited Roberts Creek, accompanying her parents in a small boat. Her father, Dr. Charles Covernton, had come to look at some property, which he subsequently purchased. For the next four summers he and his family stayed in Harry Robert's "castle" until 1924 when Dr. Covernton built his own cottage. "From then on," says Mary, "we used to come every year for the entire summer."

As a child Mary was well acquainted with the Roberts family, especially Harry. "He was quite an old boy, you know? He had a sawmill around the creek and I remember playing in the sawdust." Years later, when Mary was grown with children and grandchildren of her own, Harry gave her one of his books. In it he'd penned, "To little Mary from Roberts Creek Harry." "He remembered me as a girl," she says, still delighted.

There was no electricity during those early years and water was piped down from a part of the creek near the present Golf Club. "You put your own pipe down," remembers Mary. The five Covernton children stayed in tents behind the cottage. They were each allowed to bring a friend from Vancouver. "We used to go fishing all the time. Of course it was just rowboats and your fishing lines were just lines on a stick, but we always caught fish. You used to look out on a weekend

Mary Covernton O'Brian.

and it was just solid with boats that came from Vancouver to fish. Now you never see any. There aren't the fish, of course." She's sad for a moment, then brightens. "The wharf was a great drawing card, too. We used to sit out there and fish for shiners and cod. I think one of the nicest things for me now is when I see my grandchildren and great-grandchildren doing exactly the same things we did: going to the beach, finding crabs, building sand castles, going up the creek."

In 1967 Mary and her husband, Peter "P.D." O'Brian, purchased the land that was once the Kewpie Camp. The Legion had the property for sale and the O'Brians were afraid it might be turned into a motel. "It's right next to us and there were no regulations in this area at that point. We were getting too big for one place, so we bought the camp for our family." Mary walks around the buildings nestled beneath aging cedar and fir trees, pointing out the Castle, which now belongs to her granddaughter, and the old Merrick home that one of her daughter's is renovating. "Tom and Nancy Roberts were buried here," she says. "When he built his house, Mr. Merrick got permission to move the graves, but all that was left were the two handles from the coffins. So he scooped up what was in the place and had a little burial down at the cemetery." She continues the tour, past the Kewpie meeting hall known as the Playroom (now home to another daughter) to what was once the cookhouse. Near the park is a blue, two-storey building that used to be a barn—the first building the Kewpie's used. She points across the creek to the old Dunn property that belongs to a third daughter. "The Dunns put in

a grass tennis court. We all used it during the summer."

The property seems to draw her family back, even those who live in faraway places. "This is where their roots are, rather than the houses they grew up in." She tells of a grandson now living in Germany who recently returned to the camp with his German wife and all of her relatives for a second wedding ceremony, and of a granddaughter in the Grand Caymans who wants to return here to live. She nods at the beach stretching eastward. "All along here you'll find the same history from families that have started off camping and now they are living here, fifth generation sort of thing."

In 1975 Mary and P.D. retired to a cottage their son-in-law built for them close to the original Covernton cottage. Like many local residents, they would like to see the essence of old Roberts Creek preserved. "I don't mind people moving in here," says Mary, "as long as they appreciate the woods and water."

Barbara Paulus

On acreage just off Henry Road, a small A-frame studio is tucked among trees and flower gardens. Inside Barbara "Barby" Paulus perches on a stool surrounded by looms and cones of various fibres, from silk to mohair. Nearby, in a rainbow of colours, woven fabrics adorn display racks. A smallish woman with a gentle demeanor, she tells of her first introduction to weaving as a child in Ontario. "Every summer we would travel to our cottage, stopping on the way at Mrs. Silversides' Weaving Shop," she says. "My sister and I used to say when we grew up we were going to be weavers."

But it wasn't until she was married and living in Langley that Barby actually took lessons. "I just fell in love with it. I was a legal secretary at that time and gradually the weaving kind of took over." She attended classes at Kwantlen University College in Langley and has since participated in weaving and spinning workshops across North America, as well as taking decorating courses that included basic colour theory.

Barby chuckles as she tells about her training project with her mentor, Gwen Batchelor. "The first thing beginners usually weave is a sample, and then they do a small project. I

Barby Paulus at the Fibre Arts Festival in Gibsons.

wanted to weave a humungous rug." Although her teacher was dubious, she agreed, and eventually Barby completed the rug. "It was insane as a first project!"

Thereafter she focussed on simpler creations. She wove placemats to the point of boredom, then moved on to more complicated rugs, upholstery, and "wearable" art, before she began hand-painting her fibres. She lifts a silk scarf from the display. The soft, smooth fabric is patterned with rectangles distinguished from each other by pastel shades of mauve. "Weaving is such a tactile art," she observes, running her fingers over the material. "I love mixtures of colour and texture."

Using up to twenty pots of dyes, Barby will mix and test colours until she finds the combinations she wants; then she paints the silk or rayon fibres with a brush. When they have dried, she prepares her loom and begins to weave the fibres into a scarf—often a five-hour process—completing it with fringes. After washing, drying, and pressing, the piece is finished.

Unlike mass-produced clothing no two hand-woven garments are ever the same, and woven fabrics are more enduring. "Our tea towels probably last forever," Barby says. "Maybe drying a dish isn't the most exciting thing in the world, but if you're using a hand-woven towel, you turn it into something exciting."

Barby and her husband Karl moved to the Sunshine Coast in 1989. She joined the local Spinners and Weavers Guild and instantly made friends. "Wherever you go, weavers talk the same language," she says, describing the coast as a "friendly community where everybody seems to know each other." She likes the pace of life here and the inspiring scenery. She compensates for the limited markets on the coast by maintaining her membership in the Langley Spinners & Weavers Guild and taking her weaving to their annual sale. She also displays her material at the Festival of the Written Arts, and through the Gibsons Landing Gallery run by the Sunshine Coast Artists Co-operative, which she helped establish.

When the first Sunshine Coast Fibre Arts Festival was held in Gibsons in August 2000, Barby demonstrated scarf weaving. That September she teamed up with portrait artist Patricia Richardson Logie in a show at the Silk Purse Gallery in West Vancouver. Using Patricia's colour palette, Barby wove complementary fabrics that she draped around the paintings.

Barby doesn't like to think of a time when she won't be able to work her looms. "Even in a power outage I can keep working," she says. "And I've met women in their nineties that are still weaving. Please will I be able to do that!"

Cindy Rudolph

In a small, shingled cabin nestled among the trees bordering Smugglers Cove Provincial Park lives Cindy Rudolph, a trim, blue-eyed lady with long blond hair. At first she seems very relaxed, a woman most comfortable in blue jeans and galoshes. An intimation of the talent and passion that lies beneath this laid-back image, however, is evident in the detailed portrayals of nature gracing the walls of her tiny kitchen.

One of Cindy's first memories is of visiting her grandfather's studio when she was five years old and watching him paint intricate flowers, butterflies, and birds on cup racks and sewing boxes he'd crafted. At the age of ten she received a set of oil paints from her artist aunt, Rita Sterloff, and soon began studying and imitating the works of the French Impressionists from books at the North Vancouver, and later, Langley libraries.

As a teenager Cindy made frequent trips to the Sunshine Coast to visit the Sterloffs at their Middle Point home. There she fell in love with the diagonals she found along rocky shorelines, the colours of the vegetation, even in winter, and the pungent smell of the conifers in the summer. "If there are gods," she says, "they must live here."

Although she spent some time at art school, Cindy mostly learned by trial and error, studying the works of other artists, participating in mall shows and visiting art galleries, especially those in Europe. Awed by Rembrandt's paintings that "just seemed to glow right off the canvas,"

Cindy Rudolph displays her artwork at the Halfmoon Bay Country Fair.

she began working with light in her own art.

One day, long before she had heard of artists like Robert Bateman, Cindy realized that she could connect her passion for art with her love of nature by painting wildlife. Her work became more detailed and realistic and she began to focus on the natural environment of which she had an intimate knowledge. The pieces she now enjoys the most are those that blend the wild world with the human world—a robin at a bird feeder or a squirrel on a deck scrapping with Stellar jays.

Eight years ago Cindy began painting on driftwood as well as canvas. "The wood will almost tell you a story," she says. "Painting on canvas is a very serious work and takes a long time. Driftwood is more lyrical and whimsical and I use a great deal of artistic license. I may have a frog and a racoon on the same piece and the frog is way too big to be natural, but I figure, what the heck? It's fun."

Exhibiting her art at craft shows provides Cindy with an opportunity to escape her reclusive lifestyle, to meet with people and get feedback from them. Her favourite event is the Halfmoon Bay Country Fair.

Today Cindy ranks among the best wildlife artists in Canada, with both domestic and international sales. In 1997 Ducks Unlimited chose one of her prints for their annual provincial draw, and later that same year she participated in a benefit for the B.C. Child Foundation with some of Canada's top artists.

Many of the subjects Cindy paints come from the Creature Comfort Wildlife Care rehabilitation centre, which she runs on her ten-acre property. "I mostly rehab racoons," she says. Usually they've been brought to her as kits. For up to fourteen weeks she nurses them with a special racoon formula from the United States that costs a hundred dollars a bucket, then slowly introduces solids to their diet: snow peas, apples, salmon and salal berries, shellfish, and amphibians such as frogs, salamanders, and minnows. When the kits are able to survive on their own, she returns them to the wilderness, often taking them by boat up the local inlets.

Racoon rehabilitation costs five hundred dollars for each kit. Although she receives donations of fruit and vegetables from the produce department of Clayton's Heritage Market, and raises some money through an annual silent auction, Cindy makes up the difference from her art revenue, which is already reduced because of the time she spends caring for the young racoons. "Last summer I was doing up to 30 bottle feedings a day. There's no way I could keep painting." She's now looking for someone to share the task, but it's a commitment few people will make. "The kits are wild animals and once they're used to one handler, they won't accept anyone else coming near them ... so you're really stuck."

Cindy's dream is to develop an education program that will teach people how to live with the wild creatures that share our environment. "We have a wonderful diversity of animals on the coast. We have to live in harmony with them." The most difficult part of this, she believes, is convincing people that there is a constructive way around every environmental problem. Installing chimney caps and odourless refuse storage are good first steps.

Sitting in the kitchen of what she fondly calls her "hippie shack," surrounded by canvas and driftwood paintings of racoons and otters and birds, it is easy to see that Cindy has found her own harmony with nature and with art. "Nature is my passion," she says. "That's what I do."

John Seabrook

The year was 1970 and the airwaves were filled with freedom songs like Neil Young's "Are You Ready For The Country. John Seabrook was a 27-year-old Safeway manager in Fairfax, California who was already disillusioned with "gigantic metro complexes." Spurred on by the music, he chucked his job, hopped in his "Magic Bus" (a Volkswagen van with a pop-up roof) and headed north in search of unspoiled land.

Arriving on the Sunshine Coast he inquired about camping spots and was directed to an Egmont residence "where there's a teapot hanging on a pole." He drove into the yard just as the announcer on his radio was introducing Beethoven's Egmont Overture. "The synchronicity just blew my mind," he says. "I realized that this was the spot I was looking for ... a little oasis on the edge of a natural wilderness."

He turned a twenty dollars-a-month boatshed into a residence, and by fishing and growing most of his food, he was able to live on a small income earned by cutting and selling wood and doing odd jobs. Eventually he obtained a commercial cod licence that he used during the winter and spring. In the summer he would often crew on the big salmon boats that fished around the Queen Charlottes. After learning to scuba dive, he developed his own company,

John Seabrook in his Egmont knife-making shop with a sample of his knives (inset).

Skookum Scuba, to fish for abalone and gooey duck clams and to do commercial salvage jobs.

By the 1980s John had bought his own home in Egmont. When he wasn't fishing or diving he was helping out at the community hall, volunteering as director, secretary-treasurer, and maintenance man on the local water board, and participating in a music group. As a hobby during slack winter months he started building knives. He travelled to California to observe top knifemakers David Boye and Robert W. Loveless, but soon realized that the best way to learn the craft was simply to make one knife after another.

John dresses casually in jeans and t-shirt and he has an easy-going manner. But the collection of newly constructed knives that gleam on his bench, and the immaculateness of his shop indicate a high regard for order.

In the centre of the workroom are buffing, grinding, and cutting tools that he has invented over the years because they weren't available in local stores. The steel he uses comes from Sweden. Most of his handle material—available in 60 different colours—originates with wood fibre from Norway that is vacuum injected with a phenolic resin at a plant in Vermont. "It stabilizes the wood so you don't have to worry about cracking or checking."

At first John sold his knives by taking them on the road to craft shows such as a 400-booth exhibit at B.C. Place where he earned the Best Craftsmaker Award for his display. However, after being profiled in several newspapers and on Global Television, his knives became so popular that everything he produces now has to be ordered three to four months in advance, and knife-making has become his full-time business.

Althoug he prefers to build functional knives, John is receiving more and more orders for knives that will be kept in glass cases and never be used. Made with precious metals, their handles are fashioned from rare and expensive materials, such as linen Micarta, Mexican ironwood, or snakewood from Guyana.

John maintains he hasn't been around Egmont long enough to be called a local—that, he says, is someone who's been here for about three generations—but he feels at home in this place. "I have achieved the goal I wanted a long time ago. Living in a nice town … where your closest friends are your next-door neighbours. If they need a hand, I help them. If I need a hand, they help me. We're all watching each other's backs. It's a reciprocal thing," he says. "What you put into the community comes back to you."

Randie Tame

Driving into Randie Tame's herb farm just off Crow Road in Roberts Creek, I shift into low gear to navigate potholes in the rough dirt road. I pass a pile of hay and a garden patch with cold frames already out, although it is only the first of March. Randie and her partner are gathering winter debris and piling it into a box trailer, but as I park my car in front of their Panabode house, she walks over. She's medium height and build, with blond hair tied back in a ponytail. The sun is shining and she looks regretfully at the garden. "I don't suppose we can do the interview out here?" she asks hopefully and sighs when I tell her I need to plug in my tape recorder. "Oh well, I supposed it's time we stopped for breakfast anyway." With the air of someone who stops for very little, she leads the way past a bed of mauve crocuses.

Inside the house, while she begins preparations for the meal, I set up my recorder on a long home-built table with many chairs around it. I ask about her background and as she slices bread for toast, she tells me she is one of seven children. Born in Seattle, she moved frequently with her family, even living in Vancouver for several years before returning to Seattle. She inherited her love of gardening from her father, Joseph Morgan. "When we moved in to a new place, we dug up the lawn and planted vegetables. We all loved gardening. I started one of my first

herb gardens with my dad." She grew lavender, rosemary, chives, dill, parsley, and several kinds of mints. "We all worked in the garden together. The neighbours would come out and watch, amazed to see all these kids and dad out working there!"

In the 1960s Randie and her siblings took to the Cascades, camping through the summer months. "People who had jobs would drive back and forth and bring supplies. We just loved it. We knew this was where we wanted to raise our kids." They heard about Roberts Creek from a teacher friend who was living at Mission Point in Wilson Creek. "When we moved here we thought we would just stop off, learn some life skills, then move north." Only they fell in love with the Sunshine Coast and never did make it north.

The group bought five acres of recently logged property on Crow Road in the fall of 1970 and spent the winter gathering manure, seaweed, and leaves for compost, and clearing the land. "Then first thing in the spring we just started planting and we had fabulous gardens!"

There were twelve adults in the group, including eighteen-year-old Randie, her four brothers, her sister Diana, their mates, and a few friends. "We were called the Crow Road Commune ... In those days communes were quite common." Until they could build proper shelters they

Randie Tame in the greenhouse of her herb farm on Crow Road.

lived in tents and teepees. "We planted broccoli, peas, lettuce, cabbage, corn—all kinds of vegetables." In the fall, they canned their harvest and lived on it throughout the winter. After two years, with some of their group working outside of the farm, they were able to afford a hydro connection to the cookhouse.

At first the neighbours were wary of these strange people. "When we joined the local Community Association it was like *us* and *them* until they saw we were hard workers. Then we were their friends." Some even donated strawberry and raspberry cuttings. "We still have the strawberries—an old English variety that you can't buy anymore. They came from Mr. Bopp in lower Roberts Creek." She looked sad for a moment. "He's no longer with us."

From the beginning there was change in the commune, people coming and then leaving after finding out that utopia was more work than they expected. "People thought they could just come and move in, you know? They'd ask, 'Is this the Crow Road commune? Where's my cabin?' So we had to get tough and let people know they couldn't just come and stay here."

Although several family members do remain, it is Randie who has steadfastly worked the farm and developed the herb garden. "I was growing the herbs and I had enough to sell. People were always asking me for pieces of plants, so I started potting them up, and slowly over the years got a little bit bigger and a little bit bigger. Then I had so much stuff I started packaging it, and the business just kind of grew from there." She began to market the herbs at craft fairs and put a sign up at the bottom of Crow Road. As her supply increased she sold to local stores. "It's a lot of very hard work, but it's work I like and I was able to be home with the kids. That was my priority for years."

Randie specialized in herb blends. "A lot of people make vinegars and oils, but the dried herb blends were my trademark." Unfortunately, they were also "labour-intensive" and she now wants to concentrate on selling plants and possibly organic seed garlic. "People are aware of garlic as they've never been before, and they want to grow it," she says. "You can't often get garlic that's suitable for our climate, so if we can grow it out for a few years, they'll know it's hardy for this area." She also wants to explore more specialized herbs and making tinctures and oils, although she already has many medicinal herbs such as St. John's wort and echinacea.

Herbs thrive on the Sunshine Coast, Randie notes. "Even those less hardy, just given a little protection and thought about where you plant them, will be fine. If people do a few things right in the beginning, they'll be so pleased because herbs give such joy," she adds enthusiastically. "I mean, just the aroma, the flavour, and colours— they're all beautiful and different."

Although the soil on the Sunshine Coast is often sandy, clay, or gravel, Randie feels it is not much different from other areas and even the worst land can be built up over the years. "We have dark, loamy soil now," she grins. "It just took us thirty years to get there!" Her secret? Composting seaweed and hay.

Randie's two daughters are adults now. "Born and raised on Crow Road!" she laughs, adding that Roberts Creek is a great place to raise kids. Whether it's renovating the breakwater at the mouth of the creek or building Cliff Gilker Park, she says, Creekers work hard together. "I think it's a wonderful place to live!"

Lee Taylor and Leigh Blakey

Blue and yellow dragon kites swoop above the sandbar, dodging nylon airplanes and giant insects. Their owners manipulate strings, making the creatures dance in the wind, delighting the adults and children who have come to watch the annual Davis Bay Fun Fly.

Organized every Victoria Day weekend since 1989 by kite-builders Leigh and Lee Taylor, it has no competitions, no prizes, and no fees——just a lot of people getting together to have fun. "Our basic goal is to get people to go into their closet, find that stupid old kite that's been hanging around, and bring their kids to fly it."

Owners of the Two Lee's Studio in Halfmoon Bay, Leigh and Lee are kindred spirits" He's tall and lean, she's short and sturdy— relaxed, easy-to-talk-to folks who seem to have escaped the hurry-up-and-get-there attitudes of this era.

In 1988 the couple opened Pastimes, a store in Sechelt that specialized in educational toys. One weekend they went to Vanier Park where kite flier Ray Bethel was practising stunts. "The old guy handed me a kite and told me to try it," Lee says. "The next day I went out and spent $250 to buy a stunt kite and all the gear."

Lee Taylor at the Davis Bay Fun Fly.

He and Leigh attended a workshop at Port Townsend, Washington, where Leigh learned about painting on fabric and Lee took sewing lessons. When they came home they set up a workshop behind the toy store and began planning the first Fun Fly at Davis Bay. The weather was cold and miserable and only about one hundred and fifty people showed up, but they all had fun and wanted to do it again.

By 1994 Lee and Leigh had attended fairs and festivals across Canada and the United States, winning many competitions, including first place at the Washington State International Kite Festival. To help promote the Fun Fly, they organized a show at the Sechelt Arts Centre, featuring kites from around the world.

A year later they sold the toy store and built the Two Lee's Studio, a spacious, two-storey, high-ceilinged building that serves as both home and workshop. The studio is filled with kites they have collected. A delicate centipede kite from China hovers above a long worktable that almost traverses the room. Brightening one corner are windsocks with inlays of orcas and herons, and a saucy tugboat that Leigh playfully calls "Little Toot." Gracing the stairwell is a banner portraying mountains and an inlet with orange sunset colours relfected in the water.

Selling kites, banners, and windsocks, mostly at local craft fairs and the Farmer's Market, is not a lucrative business. Still, it suits the laid-back lifestyle they've chosen. While Lee still loves to get kites up in the air and to watch other people stunt flying, he has more fun creating and building. "The key to a good kite is proper bridling and balance," he says, but sometimes he abandons these rules in favour of creativity. Leigh likes painting—exploring colours and marbling techniques—and making banners and paper kites such as tiny tissue-paper doves with tinsel streamers.

Lee and Leigh are often found at schools and special events. While one helps kids build kites out of scraps, the other shows them how to fly their new creations. Lee loves to hand people a kite just to see the delight on their faces when they realize they can make it fly. "This is just so great!" one 80-year-old man exclaimed. "His smile made my weekend," says Lee.

Part of the couple's five-year plan is to turn the lower half of their home into guest-rooms so they can offer weekend workshops on kite building. In the meantime, they'll continue building and flying kites and organizing the Fun Fly, which now brings more than a thousand people to the shores of Davis Bay each May.

Howard and Mary White

Howard and Mary White (née Lee) are a typical Sunshine Coast couple—casually dressed, friendly, but with a touch of reserve. She's a petite redhead who manages their publishing company's office, running the computer system, and taking charge of design and production. In her spare time she plays saxophone and clarinet, performing with the Harbour Lights Band, the Sunshine Coast Band, and two Sunshine Coast orchestras. Howard is tall and sports a full beard. He spends much of his time travelling the country handling the promotion side of their business, and he's adept at crisis control, a skill he learned from his early childhood experiences at his father's logging camp on Nelson Island. "A great deal of west coast independence and inventiveness comes of people growing up in frontier environments," he says. "People had to be willing to turn their hand at anything from physical catastrophes to delivering a baby in a bunkhouse."

Howard and his two siblings lived an idyllic *Huck Finn/Treasure Island* kind of existence at the camp. They had their own quarters—one of several buildings on the site—while their parents bunked in the back of the camp cookhouse. Ignoring correspondence lessons in favour of exploring the woods and shores around Green Bay, the children gave themselves over to games of imagination, comic books, and local

Howard and Mary White
at Harbour Publishing.

folklore as told by the loggers, fishermen, and boaters who worked at or visited the camp. Evenings were often spent listening to their father read from John Steinbeck and other book club offerings.

In 1955, the children entered the regular school system at Pender Harbour where Howard graduated nine years later. He went on to study English at the University of British Columbia, then returned to Pender Harbour in 1969 and started publishing a radical newspaper dubbed *The Peninsula Voice*. The paper didn't make much money, mostly because the limited population and the ferry system meant Sunshine Coast merchants didn't have to do much advertising. To support himself Howard also worked at logging and construction jobs, leaving management of the paper to Mary Lee, a young woman from Mission whom he'd met at university.

Operating loaders and backhoes gave Howard lots of time to think, and during lulls between tasks he often scribbled his thoughts and memories onto scraps of paper. He realized that the frontier ambience of Pender Harbour—and the rest of the British Columbia coast—was rapidly disappearing, and he could see that the life-stories of the pioneers were also fading. Almost as a hobby he and Mary began collecting some of these stories, and in 1972, with a $12,000 grant from the federal Local Initiatives Program, they made the leap to magazine publishing.

With the help of friends and friends of friends, managing editor Mary Lee, and Cal "Fingers" Bailey (a hitchhiker-cum-photographer who knew all about layouts), Howard produced the first *Raincoast Chronicles* magazine, printing 3,000 copies on an offset press he had obtained from the *Vancouver Sun*. The magazine included stories of rum running, native whaling, a leper colony on D'Arcy Island, and a biography of Pender Harbour pioneer Martha Warnock. It sold out within three months, by which time he and Mary were already hard at work producing a second volume.

By 1974 Howard and Mary had ventured into book publishing with *The Dulcimer Tuning Book, Build Your Own Floor Loom,* and a *Dictionary of Chinook Jargon.* That year they launched Harbour Publishing with Peter Trower's *Between the Sky and the Splinters.* Because Howard still needed to work at construction jobs away from home, Mary continued to manage the office and to handle most of the editing and production.

The Whites were married in 1975, and that year they embarked on the riskiest venture of their careers by borrowing $15,000 to publish *Raincoast Chronicles First Five.* They were targeting the Christmas market and when the books didn't arrive from the printer until early December, Howard began flogging the collection to anyone who would listen. His self-directed promotion tour took him to the CBC *Hourglass* show where, because of a strike, he was left adlibbing on the air for fifteen minutes, unassisted by script or interviewer. The next morning orders for the book began pouring in and they soon made back their investment and a whole lot more.

Harbour's prominence increased each year, as did their list of titles by British Columbia authors and poets, and by the late 1980s Howard was able to devote himself full time to publishing. Today their annual sales are in the million-dollar range and they have a staff of eight permanent employees, including Mary who is co-publisher and partner in the firm.

Because they limit their publications to books on topics they believe in, and by writers they've come to know personally, few manuscripts are accepted over the transom and more than five hundred are returned to writers each year.

Like many of his famous Pender Harbour neighbours, Howard values his privacy and he doesn't like a lot of publicity about Harbour Publishing, a near impossibility for a company that has published more than three hundred and fifty successful books. It's also a challenge for someone who has authored and/or co-authored more than six books, who's been published in magazines such as *Macleans*, *Readers Digest*, and *B.C. Outdoors*, and who has won a multitude of awards and honours, including the Stephen Leacock Award for Humour, and the Order of B.C., which he received in 1999.

Nor has Howard's renown been limited to publishing. In 1989 he entered politics, seeking the NDP nomination for the Mackenzie Riding. "I was frustrated with the lack of interest in cultural and coastal issues in Victoria," he says. "I wanted to go there and see if I could fix that."

When he failed to win the election, Howard turned his attention to fulfilling another dream: producing the first *Encyclopaedia of British Columbia*. Written largely by historian, Daniel Francis, and aided by a board of advisors that includes Peter C. Newman, Jean Barman, Rowland Lorimer, and Barry Broadfoot, as well as the help of more than a hundred volunteers, the encyclopaedia and accompanying CD-ROM were released in October 2000. "We've been documenting B.C. in every way for 25 years, so this is a natural outgrowth of that program," says Howard. "It's everything I wanted it to be."

In 1999 Howard stepped into the local limelight once more as president of the Francis Point Marine Park Society, which promoted the recent purchase of a 70-hectare waterfront wilderness called the Francis Point Marine Park. "One of the reasons I went into politics," he admits, "was to see if I could do something to save that property. So it's been a huge satisfaction for me to have pulled it off—with a lot of help from an incredible and enthusiastic local group."

With so many dreams already achieved, it will be interesting to see what Howard's "west coast inventiveness" will lead him to next.

Violet Winegarden

Violet Winegarden lives at Happy Cat Haven in Gibsons in a house where cats roam freely except for a wire cage that protects her own tiny living/sleeping area from their intrusion. It's an unusual arrangement, but then, this lady's life has been unusual right from the very beginning.

In 1929 Dorothy Husdon died shortly after giving birth to Violet. Unable to cope with single parenthood, Henry Husdon left the newborn and his five other daughters to the care of his mother, seventy-two-year-old Georgina Husdon. She retrieved Violet from the Vancouver General Hospital, then took the steamboat to the Gibsons wharf where she was met by Doctor Fred Inglis. Lifting the blanket wrapped around the baby, he shook his head and said, "Well, don't bother to dress it, Mrs. Husdon." Whereupon Georgina grabbed the blanket from his hands, threw it back over her grandchild's face and said haughtily, "We'll see." For the next month the baby lived in a shoebox on the oven door. "She managed," Violet says admiringly.

As a child Violet attended the opening of the Roberts Creek Community Hall. She created a "snake hospital" for wounded reptiles, and was once comforted by a pod of killer whales while rowing with her sister through a storm on the Georgia Strait. When she was eleven her grandmother died and Violet went to Vancouver where she worked for

*Violet Winegarden
at her home in Gibsons.*

room and board and the chance to go to school at Lord Byng High School. "You had to do everything you were told," she remembers. "And there was always the threat that they'd throw you out."

Just after the end of the Second World War she returned to the Sunshine Coast to stay with her sisters who had opened a store and café across the highway from what is now Kern's Mall. There she met Arnold "Ted" Rikart Winegarden, a son of Emma Jane Gibson, who had died a few years earlier, and Arnold W. "Chuck" Winegarden. Violet was stealing cherries from the Winegarden trees when the door to the house opened and a man came out. He sauntered over to the tree where she was hiding, cramped and desperate, in the branches. "Isn't this a private yard?" he asked.

"Yes, but there's only an old man living here. Who are you to be asking anyway?" Violet demanded crossly, to which Ted responded, "I'm the son of that old man." It seemed Ted had just returned from overseas duty in the army.

A year later the two were married, living first in the Winegarden family home, then building their own house on School Road. It was here that they raised their two sons, Ted and Nelson, and here in the 1950s that Violet established an SPCA animal shelter. "Everyone used to throw their animals over our fence," she recalls. "We'd get up in the morning and in our yard would be dogs, cats, kittens, a skunk once, and a seal."

Today at Happy Cat Haven, which she started in 1991, Violet and a small, devoted group of volunteers tend sick, injured, and abandoned cats from all over B.C. She nurses the animals, which she refers to as "clients," has them spayed or neutered, and adopts them out, sometimes by putting their picture on the Happy Cat Haven website. Having gained an international reputation as a "kitten expert," she often gets calls from people in places such as southern California asking for advice. "There

The Husdon daughters with their grandmother Georgina Husdon: Jean and Eileen in the apple tree, Henrietta beside Mrs. Husdon, and Violet in front.

isn't anything I won't do to keep a kitten alive," she insists.

Local veterinarians offer major discounts and frequently lend a hand. "I can ask them anything," Violet says. She also speaks admiringly of the community support she receives. When one injured client needed special treatment, Violet called a neighbour requesting an aloe vera frond. The word spread and within a few hours there were seven plants left on the Happy Cat doorstep.

Funded through the sale of knitted catnip mice, garage sales, recycling, and grocery tapes, Happy Cat Haven is always searching for more money. "We all buy lottery tickets," Violet says. She has a firm conviction that one day they'll win and the shelter will be secure.

In 1999 Violet won the Golden Girl title awarded by the Gibsons Landing Heritage Society for "her caring nature, her ability to take on huge responsibilities and her generous giving to the community." Like her Grandmother Husdon, she sees what needs to be done and does it, even if others think the task is impossible. When asked recently how long she will keep Happy Cat Haven going, she laughs and says, "Till I drop."

18

Accommodation

The Sunshine Coast is gifted with a wide variety of accommodations which includes campgrounds, health retreats, hostels, hotels, motels, resorts, and RV parks. Those described in this book were selected at random and, except for the West Coast Wilderness Lodge, were visited by the author.

Further information about accommodations, "stay and play" packages, and group bookings can be obtained from <www.bigpacific.com> or from the Sunshine Coast Bed, Breakfast and Cottage Owners Association website at <www.bigpacific.com/bbsunshinecoast>.

Prices quoted are subject to change.

Langdale Heights RV and Par 3 Golf Resort

Hosts: Mike "Mick" and Gisele Chamberlin
             Michael and Mona Chamberlin
             RR #6 2170 Port Mellon Hwy, Unit 100
             Gibsons, B.C. V0N 1V6
Phone: 604-886-2182 **Toll Free** 1-800-234-7138 **Fax** 604-886-2182
E-mail: langdale_heights_rv@sunshine.net
Website: <www.langdaleheights.com>
Units: 60   **Rates:** $23/night plus GST

FEATURES: Full RV hook-up: sewer, water, electricity, telephone jack, and cablevision. Tent sites. Horseshoe pitch. Volleyball nets. Children's playground. Fire pit. Par 3 golf course.

Langdale Heights RV Park is a family-owned operation that began in 1984 when Mick and Gisele Chamberlin gave up their frontier lifestyle and moved from Bridge Lake to Gibsons where Mick established a successful excavating business.

The RV park had been built in 1989 to provide accommodation for workers involved in the Howe Sound Pulp and Paper mill reconstruction. The Chamberlins rebuilt the infrastructure, increased the number of sites, landscaped the slopes, and created a 9-hole/par 27 golf course. Swampy areas were converted into ponds and brush cleared and smoothed for greens. "We have a beautiful lay of land for a golf course," says Gisele. "Rolling hills, islands of trees, and ferns."

In addition to the golf course, the park has a store, a small golf pro shop, and a licensed coffee shop. Golf lessons are available, and there is an annual in-park tournament. A fire pit can be used for group gatherings, as well as a fully wired marquee set on a cement pad. There is also a horseshoe pitch, volleyball nets, a children's playground, and a recreation room with a large-screen television, VCR, piano, games, and easy chairs. At scheduled times movies are shown on a 100-inch movie screen.

Gabriels on Gambier Bed, Book & Breakfast

Hosts: Margaret and Leagh Gabriel
         Avalon Bay Road, Gambier Harbour
         Gambier Island, B.C. V0N 1V0
Phone: 604-886-0419
E-mail: m_gabriel@sunshine.net
Website: <www.bigpacific.com/guests/gabriels>
Units   2   **Rates:**   Low Season - $50 single $75 double
                           High Season - $65 single $85 double
                           Lunch - $10,   Dinner - $20

FEATURES: Island retreat close to secluded beaches, hiking and mountain biking trails. Cooking classes and retreats for small groups.

A former film editor for CBC, Margaret Gabriel is a collector of rare books, qualified chef, and an accomplished artist. She has studied aromatherapy and spiritual guidance and she and her husband Leagh adhere to a philosophy of simple living.

    The Gabriels' unique hexagonal home was built in the 1970s in a secluded clearing beside a small pond and an ancient old growth fir called "Norm." Huge beams, which came from a bridge on Texada Island, give the interior of the house an Elizabethan air. The Walden Room, with a double and single bed, looks out on the pond; and the Douglas Room has two twin beds and overlooks the meadow. A common bathroom is located between the two rooms. Guests are welcome to share the Gabriel's sunken living area that is furnished with comfortable chairs and contains a large television and stereo. Throughout the home are shelves of books for reading or buying.

    Breakfast is a three-course meal with free-range eggs, home-baked bread, muffins, and pastries. An English tea of fresh scones and cake is served in the afternoon. Lunches and dinners are provided at an additional cost, and vegan or vegetarian meals are available on request.

Bonniebrook Lodge Bed & Breakfast

Hosts: Karen and Philippe Lacoste
1532 Oceanbeach Esplanade
RR #5, Gibsons, B.C. V0N 1V5
Phone: 604-886-2887 **Fax:** 604-886-8853
E-mail: info@bonniebrook.com
Website: <www.bonniebrook.com>
Units: 40 Campsites **Rates:** $17 per night un-serviced sites
$20 per night with electricity & water
Based on 1 tent and 2 adults at site

7 Suites Main Lodge second floor: $145-$180
Main Lodge penthouse: $125-$160
Creekside Romance Suite: $110-$140

FEATURES: Historic ocean-side lodge and tent and RV campsite in park-like setting. Chez Philippe Restaurant specializing in French cuisine.

Bonniebrook has been a vacation spot since 1912 when J.S. Chaster and his wife began renting cottages and campsites on their homestead. The Chasters would row from the beach to the Union Steamships to pick up or discharge guests. When fire destroyed the original lodge in 1929, their son Harry built the one that exists today. In 1946 the G.T. Williams family renovated the lodge and built the stone fireplace in the dining room.

Present owners Philippe and Karen Lacoste are both qualified chefs. He trained in a Parisian restaurant before immigrating to Canada, and she apprenticed at Jean Pierre's Restaurant in Vancouver. Together they have transformed Bonniebrook into a modern lodge with an old world atmosphere. Roomy suites have queen-sized beds

and a sitting area. Jacuzzi tubs are set beneath "art" windows. Breakfast is brought to the suites or served in the main dining room. Verandahs offer ocean views and across the street is Chaster Park where visitors can often spot deer, otters, herons, and eagles.

Marina House Bed & Breakfast

Hosts: Sue and Gordon Bailey
546 Marine Drive,
Gibsons, B.C. V0N 1V0
Phone: (604) 886-7888 **Toll Free:** 1-888-568-6688
E-mail: marinahouse@sunshine.net
Website: <www.bbregistry.com/ca/Marina_House_Bed_Breakfast.htm>
Units: 3   **Rates:** $95-$110

FEATURES: Heritage building close to shops, seawall, and swimming. Private entrance. Friendly hosts who love to cook.

Located beside the harbour seawall, Marina House was completed in 1931 by Gibsons' pioneer, Dr. Fred Inglis and his sons. "Jack Inglis told us it took them about seventeen years to build," says present owner Sue Bailey. She points out the birds-eye maple used on the doorjambs. "I think Dr. Inglis milled it himself."

From the verandah in front of the common dining/living area guests can sit and watch the activity of the harbour: tugboats nudging a barge to the landing, sailboats heading for a Sunday morning regatta, seals splashing in the water, and seagulls, cormorants, and grey herons perched on logs or pilings.

The rooms are small but cosy, with hardwood floors and antique furnishings. Breakfast is served in the dining area, and features poached egg with smoked salmon and lemon sauce, fresh fruit, scones, and muffins. Specialties are a five-pepper frittata or stuffed French toast.

The seawall provides an easy, picturesque walk to Armours Beach—a popular swimming spot for local residents—or to the Gibsons Wharf and Winegarden Park.

Captain Craddock's Bed & Breakfast

Hostess: Joan Craddock
305 Cochrane Road
Gibsons, B.C. V0N 1V8
Phone: 1-800-886-3308
E-mail: captaincraddocks@dccnet.com
Website: <www.bbcanada.com/captaincraddocks>
Units: 2 **Rates:** Contact host.

FEATURES: Family and fisherman friendly lodging in Gibsons Landing.

When her Vancouver accounting job was phased out, Joan Craddock decided to make use of her natural skills as a hostess and enhance her enjoyment of people by opening a bed and breakfast. The duplex that she and her husband Chris had purchased in the late 1980s provided a perfect location within walking distance of two museums, art galleries, restaurants, shops—including those in Molly's Reach—the seawall, beaches, and swimming.

The bedrooms (queen/private, twin/ensuite) are roomy and comfortably furnished, and there is a common sitting room with a small library, cable TV, and games drawer. While a full breakfast menu is offered, Joan's specialty is blueberry pancakes. For those who choose to self-cater there is a spacious kitchen that has a fridge, stove, and microwave. Outside is a large deck with barbeque and a garden patio with fire pit.

Sunshine Coast Country Hide-Away

Hosts: Gunter and Marcelina Beyser
1148 Reed Road RR#7
Gibsons, B.C. V0N 1V7
Phone: 604-886-7261 **Fax:** 604-886-7261
E-mail: gbeyser@hotmail.com
Website: <www.countryhideaway.bigstep.com>
Units: 2 **Rates:** $60 single $65 double, additional person $20

FEATURES: Quiet country acreage with spacious lawns and flower gardens. Private entrance. TV/VCR.

Gunter and Marceline Beyser immigrated from Germany and the Philippines. When their three children were grown the couple turned their home into a bed and breakfast.

The bedrooms are bright and clean and have ensuite bathrooms. A large covered deck facing the front garden is warmed on cool days by an overhead heater. Guests can enjoy their breakfasts here, amid the weeping lace maple and climbing roses, or in the family dining area. "I have five different breakfasts," Marcelina says. "If people stay a week, they get a different breakfast and a different table setting every day." Menus include fresh strawberries and raspberries from their garden (in season) and homemade preserves.

Unique gardens, fruit trees, and evergreens surround the Beyser's home. "I think we have at least 50 different species of trees," says Gunter. "We have a lot of rhododendrons. I grow all of my annuals from seed—wax begonias, geraniums, impatience, marigolds—I have them by the thousands." Near the house a small gazebo offers a quiet nook for reading or meditating.

Rosewood Country House

Hosts: Susan Berryman Tonne and Frank Tonne
RR #5 575 Pine Street
Gibsons, B.C. V0N 1V5
Phone: 604-886-4714 **Fax:** 604-886-8119
E-mail: rosewood@uniserve.com
Website: <www.rosewoodcountryhouse.com>
Units: 2 **Rates:** $195 (Canadian)

FEATURES: Destination bed and breakfast in old English country house setting. Large ponds, bridged gazebo, gardens, and waterfowl. Ocean view.

Frank and Susan Tonne designed and built a 1910 Craftsman-style home, using lumber milled from their own trees. Each room has a story such as the leaded glass doors rescued from an old home in Shaughnessy and a tin ceiling from the Eldorado Hotel in Kelowna.

Furnished with antiques and decorated with paintings and sculptures by local artists, Rosewood has an old-fashioned elegance. A games room contains a snooker table, dartboard, musical instruments, and videos. Both guest rooms offer a queen-sized bed, ensuite, private entrance, TV, VCR, and fireplace. The Sunset Suite has an ocean view, while the Garden Suite, complete with spa bath and stained glass, looks out onto the gardens. Open and covered decks provide quiet nooks and a dining area for breakfasts or sunset dinners. Breakfasts that range from traditional egg and sausage dishes to Susan's unique French toast are served with champagne and flowers.

Rosewood is graced with lawns, flowerbeds, and fishponds frequented by herons, mallards, and blue jays. Two arched bridges lead to a gazebo in the centre of the largest pond—a favourite spot for wedding photos.

Moon Cradle Backpackers Retreat

Hostess: Shaeah Fialkow
3125 Highway 101, RR #2
Roberts Creek, B.C. V0N 2W2
Phone: 604-885-2070 **Fax:** 604-885-6640
E-mail: hello@mooncradle.com
Website: <www.mooncradle.com>
Units: 2 4-person dorms **Rates:** $22-$55

FEATURES: Clean, comfortable hostel with environmental theme and vegetarian cuisine. Wood-burning sauna.

Moon Cradle is a five-bedroom home transformed into a hostel modelled on those Shaeah stayed in during world travels. In each guest room are two unique sets of bunks made of driftwood (from the Roberts Creek beach) and locally milled cedar. On the same level are a recreation area, kitchenette, bathroom, and laundry.

Continental breakfast with organic juice, muffins, and granola is served at a unique, handcrafted dining table upstairs. Guests are welcome to use the kitchen, but are requested not to cook meat except on the outside fire pit.

Located within easy hiking distance of the beach and three parks, as well as the Mt. Elphinstone trail system, Moon Cradle also offers kayak and snowshoe rentals. Having studied Shaitsu and Japanese thumb pressure, Shaeah will provide tired guests with a free shoulder massage, or a full massage for an extra fee. Guests are welcome to participate in weekly yoga sessions and drum workshops run by local percussionists.

The Willows Inn

Hosts: John and Donna Gibson
3440 Beach Avenue
Roberts Creek, B.C. V0N 2W0
Phone: 604-885-2452 **Fax:** 604-885-5872
E-mail: donna_gibson@dccnet.com
Units: 1 **Rates:** May-Oct $110 double $95 single
Off season: $95 double $85 single
Package deals available.

FEATURES: Quiet, secluded cottage, close to the beach and the heart of Roberts Creek; complimentary golf passes.

As the grandson of Lockyer Road homesteaders, and a life-long resident of Roberts Creek, John Gibson is well acquainted with local landmarks. His wife, Donna, has spent years in the hospitality industry and works as a hostess at the Driftwood Inn. Together they have built a dream cottage, tucked beneath tall cedars and sheltered from view by a vine-covered fence. Inside the cottage is a double bed, a full bathroom, and kitchen area with sink, fridge, microwave, and cable TV. A small wood heater augments electric heat.

"We believe in spoiling people," Donna says. "We bring breakfast over when our guests want it, rather than at a set time." Her specialty is chocolate-coated strawberries, developed to keep the berries in her fruit baskets looking fresh. Now they're the first thing returning guests ask for.

Welcome Inn

Hosts: Mike and Joan Weiner
General Delivery, 1176 Flume Road
Roberts Creek, B.C. V0N 2W0
Phone: 604-740-0318 or 1-800-986-0001   **Fax:** 604-740-0318
E-mail: welcome_inn@sunshine.net
Website: <www.sunshine.net/www/1200/sn1281/>
Units: 4   **Rates:** $60 - $100

FEATURES: Wrap-around verandah that looks out onto beautiful gardens and hanging baskets. Year-round creek. Close to the beach and provincial park.

Mike and Joan Weiner emigrated from South Africa in 1986 and started the successful Procope restaurant in Vancouver and a few years later, the Cornucopia. In 1996 they moved to Roberts Creek and remodelled their newly purchased home into a picturesque bed and breakfast inn. Guest rooms are clean and bright with colour schemes to match their flowery names. Each has a private bath with shower. A fully furnished two-bedroom cottage is also available, complete with its own yard, lawn chairs, and barbecue.

    Breakfast is served in the dining room and typically includes juice, cereal, "sozzled" grapefruit, croissants or hot cross buns, and an entrée. Afternoon tea is served on the verandah between 4:00 and 5:00 p.m. "Everyone brings the treasures they've found and share experiences," says Joan. In the evening the guests can relax in a cosy sitting room and help themselves to complimentary tea or coffee.

Eagle View Bed and Breakfast

Hosts: Victor and Cecelia Walker
4839 Eagleview Road
Davis Bay, Sechelt, B.C. V0N 3A2
Phone: 604-885-7225   **Fax:** 604-885-7208
E-mail: eagleview_b&b@sunshine.net
Website: <www.pixsell.bc.ca/bcbbd/2/2000459.htm>
Units: 2   **Rates:** $45 - $70

FEATURES: Bright, modern house with ocean view. Close to beach. Private entrance. Free VCR movies.

Victor Walker was an English sea captain who worked along the China Coast and later as a harbour master in Trinidad. Cecelia came to Canada with an English family as a nanny. They moved to the Sunshine Coast in 1971, where Victor worked as a captain with BC Ferries until he retired in 1986.

Eagle View is situated on a hill overlooking Georgia Strait. Guest bedrooms are downstairs and connect to a sitting room with gas fireplace, TV and VCR, and a large deck. Flower gardens are accentuated with shells, driftwood, and glass floats that they have collected on their travels along the Pacific coast. In the garage is a collection of shells and agates from all over the world.

"We enjoy having guests," says Victor. "We like to treat them as friends and tell them as much as we can about the coast and the things there are to do."

Breakfast is served in the family dining area and guests can choose from a menu that includes pancakes, homemade bread, muffins and jam, fruit, cereal, a variety of egg, ham, and sausage dishes.

Sunset Beach Bed and Breakfast

Hosts: Janice and Lee Brown
            5231 Sunshine Coast Hwy 101
            Sechelt, B.C. V0N 3A2
Phone: 604-885-7006
E-mail: lbrown@sd46.bc.ca
Units: 2   **Rates:**   up to $100

FEATURES: Private entrance and ocean-side deck. Ground floor suites; ensuite bathrooms; gas fireplace; TV; VCR; kitchenette; barbeque. Beach suitable for swimming or walking. Close to town centre.

Janice and Lee Brown have been teaching on the Sunshine Coast since 1980. They started their first bed and breakfast in 1999, enjoying the experience so much that when they rebuilt a year later they included two specially designed bed and breakfast suites on the ground floor.

Both suites contain a queen-sized bed, ensuite bathroom, gas fireplace, sitting area with fold-out couch, and a kitchenette. Each has a private, covered deck with barbeque, table and chairs, and provides a sunset view of Georgia Strait and the Trail Islands. A rocky beach fronting the house allows for easy walking and swimming, and at low tide a sandbar is exposed that connects to the Davis Bay sandbar. Kayaks are available for guests to use on the water.

Janice and Lee will carry luggage to and from the upland parking area. Janice provides newly arrived guests with an evening basket that contains a bottle of wine and a snack. Hearty, organic continental-style breakfasts are served in the suite and include organic fruits (in season), yoghurts, muffins, bread, and freshly ground regular or decaffeinated coffee.

Shoreline Place Bed and Breakfast

Hosts: Liane and Andrew Hansen
               6550 Gale Road North
               Sechelt, B.C. V0N 3A5
Phone: 604-740-0767   **Fax:** 604-740-0767
Website: <www.bigpacific.com/guests/shoreline>
Units: 1 2-bedroom suite **Rates:** $130-150 Family rates available.

FEATURES: Private entrance, near beach. Hot tub. Families welcome.

Liane and Andrew fell in love with the Sunshine Coast while they were camping at Porpoise Bay Park. When they returned home to North Vancouver where Liane was a triathalon coach and bike safety instructor and Andrew was a building contractor, they decided they wanted to move here permanently. They purchased property on the west side of Porpoise Bay and began drawing plans for a new house that they built and landscaped together.

Located on the lower floor, the bedrooms are bright and comfortable, with one queen and two twin beds and a private bathroom. A large sitting room contains comfy loveseats and a gas fireplace, and offers a breathtaking view of Sechelt Inlet and the Tetrahedron mountains. Guests can relax on the patio, cook a steak on the barbeque, soak in the hot tub, or stroll around Liane's flower gardens. A short trail leads down to a sandy swimming beach. "It's a great place for children," Liane says.

For breakfast she likes to give her guests whatever they want, and often they choose items that previous visitors have enthused about in the guest book. "Last year it was my blackberry pancakes. Now it's the shrimp omelette." Besides the entrée, fresh bread, muffins, and fruit salad are always available.

Tranquility Bay Bed & Breakfast

Hosts: Chris and Krista Cutlan
7651 Sechelt Inlet Road
Sechelt, B.C. V0N 3A4
Phone: 604-885-3442 **Toll Free:** 1-800-665-2311 **Fax:** 604-885-9038
E-mail: info@tranquilitybay-bc.com
Website: <www.tranquilitybay-bc.com>
Units: 2   **Rates:** $119 - $139

FEATURES: New cabin and lodge along the shores of Sechelt Inlet; outdoor sitting nooks; campfire area; Sundance therapeutic spa; mountain bike and kayak rentals; recreation room.

Krista spent many summer vacations on this long time family property in Tuwanek. A few years ago she and Chris moved there from Kelowna and built a large alpine-style lodge with a bed and breakfast suite on the lower floor. The unit has a separate entrance and includes an ensuite bathroom, chiropractic bed, and sitting room. Closer to the beach they added a one-bedroom knotty pine cabin with a sitting area, breakfast nook, and bathroom.

Guests of the suite have a recreation room with a wet bar, pool table, organ, 52-inch home theatre, DVD movies, exercise equipment, and a massage table; or they can soak in the therapeutic spa outside. A deck near the water provides an excellent view of inlet sunsets.

Krista serves a full, multi-course breakfast with fresh fruit, muffins, croissants, beverages, and an entrée such as Belgian waffles, eggs Benedict with ham or smoked salmon, or her specialty—baked apple pancakes.

Pacific Shores Bed and Breakfast

Hostess: Dorothy Dolphin
5853 Sunshine Coast Highway, Box 614
Sechelt, B.C. V0N 3A0
Phone: 604-885-8938 **Fax:** 604-885-8938
E-mail: pacshrs@aol.com
Units: 1 **Rates:** $115 - $130

FEATURES: Private entrance. Large suite with fireplace, sitting area, and ensuite bathroom. Patio. Georgia Strait view.

The waterfront home Dorothy Dolphin purchased in 1991 is situated on the site where Sechelt's first European settler, Thomas John Cook, built his original cabin in 1893. "The grove of trees that surrounded his cabin still exists," she says. "The foundation to his second house is still present on the beach." As a child, Dorothy and her family spent a portion of their summer holidays visiting her Aunt Mabel and Uncle Charles McDermid at their logging camp on Sechelt Inlet. Arriving on the Union Steamship they would stop at the Village Café for sodas before walking to Porpoise Bay to meet the camp boat.

Large windows in the bed and breakfast suite provide an ocean view. A door opens onto the garden and fish pond. Near the beach an easy trail leads to Snickett Park and the Trail Bay promenade. Within a five-minute walk are the shops and restaurants of Sechelt.

Dorothy offers her guests a breakfast of croissants or homemade muffins, fresh squeezed orange juice, a fruit plate and an entrée such as crepes, omelette, or French toast. She will serve it in the suite or on the patio.

Tucker's Inn

Hosts:	Diaya and Peter Maseja
	6966 Sunshine Coast Highway
	West Sechelt, B.C. V0N 3A8
Phone:	604-885-9077 **Toll-Free:** 1-877-266-9567
E-mail:	tuckers_inn@sunshine.net
Website:	<www.sunshine.net/www.2200/sn2277/>
Units:	2 **Rates:** $85 to $110

FEATURES: Queen-sized Posturepedic beds. Ocean view. Fireplace. Hot tub and barbecue. Private entrance.

Originally from the Czech Republic, Peter and Diaya moved to the coast from Calgary where Peter had worked at the same restaurant for over 24 years. Wanting to be at home with their children, they searched for a home-based business and found Tucker's Inn. Newly built, with twelve-foot ceilings, the inn offers a view of Georgia Strait from both bed and breakfast suites, which connect to a kitchenette, and dining and sitting area with a fireplace. Television and VCR is available, and guests are welcome to use the hot tub and barbecue on the deck. A creek runs through the property. Deer can often be seen nibbling the rose bushes planted near the patio, especially in February and March.

Breakfasts are served in the dining area or out on the patio. Diaya and Peter share the cooking, offering their guests a choice of beverages, hot or cold cereal, a fresh fruit plate with yoghurt, and an entree such as a Spanish omelette or Belgian waffles. In the afternoon Diaya serves tea in the sitting area, with homemade cookies, banana bread, or Czech baking.

The Adventure Hut

Hosts: Brad and Loraine Proctor
7755 Redrooffs Road, RR1 Eureka Site, C83
Halfmoon Bay, B.C. V0N 1Y0
Phone: 604-885-4888 **Toll Free**: 1-877-322-4888 **Fax**: 604-885-4889
E-mail: info@bikingontheedge.com
Website: <www.bikingontheedge.com>
Units: 2 bedrooms and a sleeping loft.
Rates: $100-$120 up to 5 people. Call for other rates.

FEATURES: New, self-contained cottage. Quiet, country setting. Close to hiking, mountain biking trails, and beaches. Family friendly.

In the 1980s Brad Proctor owned a bicycle frame-building business in Edmonton and was involved in competitive road and track cycling. When he and Loraine moved to the Sunshine Coast in 1993 they decided to share their passion for mountain biking with others by offering lessons in bike riding and repairs, and by giving guided tours of local trails. In 2000 they added the Adventure Hut to their program.

The hut contains a sleeping loft, two private bedrooms, laundry facilities, common bathroom and shower, a gas fireplace and a fully equipped kitchen. "We encourage guests to do their own cooking," says Loraine. "For a small extra charge, however, I will provide muffins or scones." Guests can also wander through Loraine's beautifully creative gardens, sampling raspberries, apples, pears, or plums in season.

Mountain bikers have access to a shop next to the hut for cleaning their bikes and minor repairs. Mountain bikes are also available for renting.

Beaver Island Inn & Pender Chief Charters

Hosts: Chris Kluftinger and Diane Jackson
R.R. #1, S4 C6
Madeira Park, B.C. V0N 2H0
Phone: 604-883-2990
E-mail: beaver_island_inn@sunshine.net
Website: <www.monday.com/beaverislandb&b/>
Units: 2 (3-bedroom cabin with additional hide-a-bed and a 2-bedroom cabin.)
Rates: $119 - $349 for full packages

FEATURES: Self-contained cabins; common dining room with ocean view; dock and rowboat; shade trees. Families welcome.

Chris Kluftinger trained as a chef in Germany and Switzerland. He and Diane Jackson owned a restaurant in Steveston before moving to the Sunshine Coast where Chris acquired certification as a diving instructor and was soon operating his own dive charter business. When he and Diane built the main house they turned their two cabins into bed and breakfast units.

Complete with microwave, fridge, and stove, both cabins are clean, bright, and comfortably furnished. One cabin contains a drying room for dive gear. Outside are spacious lawns, fruit trees, flower gardens, and animals: pygmy goats, a pot-bellied pig, chickens, dogs, cats, and a parrot.

Breakfasts are served in the main house, either in the dining room or on the deck and for an extra fee guests can arrange for picnic lunches, or gourmet dinners.

Package deals can be arranged that combine the bed and breakfast and dive charters, with or without equipment provided.

A remotely operated camera provides a preview of dive sites. Chris will also work as an underwater guide.

The Otters' Raft

Hosts:	Louise and David Twentyman
	13219 Dames Road
	Irvings Landing, Garden Bay, B.C. V0N 1S0
Phone:	604-883-1199
E-mail:	theottersraft@dccnet.com
Website:	<www.monday.com/ottersraft>
Units: 1	**Rates:** $120

FEATURES: Roomy cottage. Private deck near the water. Hot tub.

The Sunshine Coast's first hotel built by Charles Irvine before 1891 is only steps away from The Otter's Raft, owned by Nabob Company retirees Louise and David Twentyman. Besides supplying local establishments with freshly roasted specialty coffees, the couple also have a gourmet tea business and have recently launched a new website: <www.twentymantea.com>.

In 1999 they turned their guest cottage into a bed and breakfast unit. It has a queen-sized bed in the bedroom, a sofa bed in the sitting room, and a full kitchen. "I provide a breakfast hamper for self-catering," says Louise. "A little basket that has eggs, bacon, yoghurt, bagels, granola, fruit, orange juice, tea, and freshly roasted coffee. Then I bring fresh croissants and scones at whatever time they request." For weekly rentals, no breakfast is supplied, but the rates are reduced.

A hot tub with a private entrance for guests is located in a room with floor-to-ceiling windows that face the sea. On the rocks near the water is a deck from which they can watch the setting sun or glimpse a doe that swims from one of the small islands in search of water. Every day an eagle arrives in screeching splendour to snatch scraps from the rocks.

Ruby Lake Resort

Hosts: Antonio, Gabriella, Aldo, and Giorgio Cogrossi
           R.R. #1, Site 20, C-25
           Madeira Park, B.C. V0N 2H0
Phone: 604-883-2269 **Fax:** 604-883-3602
E-mail: talk2us@rubylakeresort.com
Website: <rubylakeresort.com>
Units: 10   **Rates:** $75 - $109

FEATURES: Modern suites; carports; bird sanctuary; playground; canoe rentals; swimming; and prize-winning Italian seafood restaurant.

Built in 1950, Ruby Lake Resort is now owned by the Cogrossi family who emigrated from Italy in the early 1990s. Chef Aldo Cogrossi transformed the lagoon into a nature preserve, planting trees and building birdhouses everywhere. Today more than 180 species of birds can be sighted at the lake, as well as turtles, beaver, otters, deer, and bear. Every afternoon an eagle that Aldo rescued returns to visit him and puts on a natural show.

A floating bridge across the lagoon connects the restaurant to the accommodations, which can also be accessed directly from the highway. Units contain full washrooms, complimentary coffee, and colour TV with free HBO; some include kitchenettes. Each unit has a carport and outdoor picnic table. Nearby is a large gazebo.

In the dining room is a display of heirlooms from the Cogrossi family estate, including antique chandeliers, a 200-year-old alabaster eagle, a 100-year-old mechanical organ, and the family crest. A fireplace warms the room on chilly nights, while the Cogrossis' hospitality warms the hearts of their customers.

Malaspina Ranch Resort

Hostess: Robina "Robi" Petraschuk
Box 29, RR #1
Madeira Park, B.C. V0N 2H0
Phone: 604-883-1122
Units: 3   **Rates:** $55 - $95 including taxes

FEATURES: Trail rides; mountain bike rentals; canoes; hot tub; pool.

Malaspina Ranch began as a 200-man logging camp started in the 1920s by Sunshine Coast pioneer Louis Heid, who built the barn that is still being used. Robi and her late husband Bill purchased the property in 1962 and turned it into a ranch, raising cattle and horses, and taking people out on trail rides. Bill also logged at Dead Dog Bay in Jervis Inlet.

The couple built the house, using teredo-sculpted timbers from his logging camp, and hundred-year-old fir flooring that had been milled at the Hastings Sawmill. When Bill died Robi sold the horses and in 1986 she opened the house as a bed and breakfast.

Located upstairs the bedrooms are clean, bright, and homey. One has an adjoining bathroom, while the other two share a bathroom down the hall. There is a large sitting room downstairs with a stone fireplace. A dining nook faces the tidal flats of East Pender Bay and French doors lead to a deck with a hot tub, and to a lower patio with a small swimming pool. For breakfast Robi prepares a fruit salad, yoghurt, home-baked bread and buns, English crumpets, apricot cake, and homemade jams. Her entrée is usually an egg dish and hashbrowns cooked with bacon and onions.

Robi's son Andy runs a mountain bike rental, repair, and guide service, and recently her son re-established the guided trail rides.

Sundowner Inn

Hosts: Colin and Anne Read
               Box 133
               Garden Bay, B.C. V0N 1S0
Phone: 604-883-9676   **Toll Free:** 888-2888-8780
E-mail: info@sundowner-inn.com
Website: <www.sundowner-inn.com>
Units: 11   **Rates:** $49 to $94. Package deals available.

FEATURES: Conference room, museum, wedding chapel, and restaurant. Kayak and bike rentals. Hot tub. Transportation from Vancouver airport.

Colin and Anne Read live in Alaska where he is a professor of economics and she is the general manager of an ecology firm. They purchased the Sundowner Inn in 1999.

Located on Hospital Bay, the inn began as the twelve-bed hospital St. Mary's Hospital opened by the Columbia Coast Mission August 16, 1930. The chapel was built and consecrated by Canon Alan Greene ten years later.

The rooms at the inn all have cable TV and a view of Hospital Bay. An exercise room is available, as well as a hot tub and lots of deck space. The chapel-museum can be used for weddings, and the conference room has modern audio visual equipment, computers, and internet facilities.

Just a few steps away is John Henry's Marina, an eclectic complex that includes a general store, liquor outlet, and woodworking shop. Many local festivals are held here, such as the August Hospital Bay Days, which include a craft fair, and dinghy boat races.

Bathgate General Store and Marina Cottages

Hosts: Doug and Vicki Martin
6781 Bathgate Road
Egmont, B.C. V0N 1N0
Phone: 604-883-2222   **Fax:** 604-883-2750
E-mail: bathgate_egmont@sunshine.net
Website: <www.bathgate.com>
Units: 2 6-person cabins   **Rates:**   Contact owners.

FEATURES: Marina, laundromat, Government Liquor Agency, and grocery store. Fuel dock. Mobile mechanic and marine ways (up to 40 tons). Boat rentals. Tent and motorhome campsites. Video rentals.

Doug and Vicki Martin retired from their Toronto banking careers in 1988 and purchased the Bathgate store and marina. They built a new workshop and hired a marine mechanic, rebuilt all of the docks, put in new double-walled gas tanks, and upgraded the laundry facilities. A sewage treatment plant was installed and the cabins renovated and refurnished. More recently they have been landscaping the property, paving the driveway and creating rock gardens.

Throughout the improvements the store has maintained its country atmosphere, with oiled fir floors and a sales inventory that ranges from groceries and fishing tackle to marine charts and hardware.

Each cabin has a fridge, stove, microwave, TV, and VCR. Nearby is a Doukhobor-styled keyhole fire pit, and just down the street is a tennis court and playground. The cabins are within hiking distance of Skookumchuck Narrows Provincial Park, and only a few hours by boat from Princess Louisa Inlet.

West Coast Wilderness Lodge

Hosts: Paul and Patti Hansen
Maple Road,
Egmont, B.C. V0N 1N0
Phone: 604-883-3667
E-mail: Camping@wcwl.com
Website: <www.wcwl.com>
Units: 20 family units **Rates:** $70 - $110 meals and accommodation

FEATURES: Outdoor adventures: kayaking, canoeing, rock climbing, ropes course. Sauna; hot tub; games room; satellite TV and VCR.

Paul Hansen spent over twenty years running outdoor educational and recreational programs. When he and Patti found their Egmont property in 1997, they realized they had a recreational paradise right in their own back yard.

They built a lodge large enough to contain twenty family units, dining facilities, a lounge area, and games room. Windows that stretch to a 40-foot peak provide a breathtaking view of Hotham Sound, Jervis and Sechelt Inlets. A hot tub is located on an enormous deck that fronts the building.

Besides offering first class cuisine and accommodations, the Hansens and their staff work hard to provide guests with an unforgettable holiday. Activities available include guided ocean kayaking, rock climbing, eco tours, and wildlife and bird watching. Designed for all age levels, the lodge is ideal for group retreats, workshops, and weddings. During the summer special family programs are available.

Every year the lodge hosts the Egmont Summer Music Festival attracting musicians from all parts of North America. Seven pianos are brought in, and practise concerts are performed on the deck.

Appendix 1

Books About the Sunshine Coast

Anderson, Doris. *The Columbia is Coming!* Sidney, BC: Gray's, 1982.

Armitage, Dorothy. *Around the Sound: A History of Howe Sound-Whistler.* Madeira Park, BC: Harbour, 1977.

Barker, Terry. *Sunshine Sketches: An Artist's History of B.C.'s Beautiful Sunshine Coast.* Self-published, 2001.

Beaumont, Ronald C. "She Shashishalhem: The Sechelt Language" *Language, Stories and Sayings of the Sechelt Indian People of British Columbia.* Theytus Books, 1985.

Blanchet, M. Wylie. *The Curve of Time.* Sidney, BC: Gray's, 1980.

Calhoun, Bruce. *Mac and the Princess; The Story of Princess Louisa Inlet.* Seattle: Ricwalt, 1976.

Campone, Merv. *Adventures on the Sunshine Coast.* Toronto: NC Press, 1981.

Carson, Bryan. *Sunshine & Salt Air: A Recreation Guide to the Sunshine Coast Revised and Updated.* Madeira Park, BC: Harbour, 1991.

Cramond, Mike. *Salmon Fishing British Columbia Vol 2: Mainland Coast.* Surrey: Heritage, 1990.

Dawe, Helen. *Helen Dawe's Sechelt.* Madeira Park, BC: Harbour, 1990.

Drope, Dorothy and Bodhi. *Paddling the Sunshine Coast.* Madeira Park, BC: Harbour, 1997.

Dubois, Florence. *William Jeffries & Other Pioneers of the Sunshine Coast and Memoirs of William Jeffries Great Granddaughter.* Elphinstone Pioneer Museum: unpublished manuscript, 1996.

Fraser, Kaari and Barbara Fraser Tilley. *Camp Olave: A History.* Camp Olave Management Committee, April 1977.

Greenfield, Tony. *The Trails of the Lower Sunshine Coast: A comprehensive guide.* Second edition. B.C. Forest Service.

Hadley, Michael L. *God's Little Ships: A History of the Columbia Coast Mission.* Madeira Park, BC: Harbour, 1995.

Haras, Willie. *Wings Across Georgia Strait: A Blue Heron Guide to Birds of East Vancouver Island, The Sunshine Coast, Islands of the Georgia Strait.* Lindsay Press, 1995.

Hill, Beth. *Upcoast Summers*. Ganges, BC: Horsdal & Schubart, 1985.

Keller, Betty and Leslie, Rosella. *Bright Seas, Pioneer Spirits*. Victoria: Horsdal & Schubart, 1996.

Keller, Betty and Leslie, Rosella. *Sea Silver: Inside British Columbia's Salmon-Farming Industry*. Victoria: Horsdal & Schubart, 1996.

Kennedy, Ian. *Guide to Neighborhood Pubs In Greater Vancouver, The Fraser Valley, Squamish, Whistler and on the Sunshine Coast*. Vancouver: Soules, 1983.

McDowell, Jim. *Warpings along the Sunshine Coast*. Gibsons: self-published, 1992.

Percheson, Rita, Pam Gross, and Sandy Barrett. *Hiking Trails of the Sunshine Coast*. Edmonds, Wa: Signpost, 1979.

Peterson, Lester Ray. *The Gibson's Landing Story*. Ottawa: Peter Martin, 1962.

Poole, Michael. *Romancing Mary Jane : a year in the life of a failed marijuana grower*. Vancouver: Greystone, 1998.

Priest, Simon. *Bicycling Southwestern British Columbia & the Sunshine Coast*. Vancouver: Douglas & McIntyre, 1985.

Roberts Creek Historical Committee, *Remembering Roberts Creek, 1889-1955*. Madeira Park: Harbour, 1978.

Robers, Fred. *Shipwrecks of British Columbia*. North Vancouver: J.J. Douglas, 1973.

Sinclair, Bertrand W. *Poor Man's Rock*. Cambridge: Little Brown & Co., 1920.

Southern, Karen. *The Nelson Island Story*. Surrey, BC: Hancock House, 1987.

Taylor Grace, Wendy Rogers, and Lauren Armstrong, *Sunshine Coast Seafood: a collection of recipes using locally available seafood*. Halfmoon Bay: Arbutus Bay Publications, 1985.

Therien, Kelly, editor. *Our Sunshine Coast: Historical Sketches*. Sechelt: SunCoast Writers Forge, 1990.

Therien, Kelly, editor. *Our Sunshine Coast, Vol II: People, Places & History*. Sechelt: SunCoast Writers' Forge, 1994.

Thomson, James R. *A Coast Childhood Remembered*. West Vancouver: self-published, 1999.

Tickner, Florence. *Fish Hooks & Caulk Boots*. Madeira Park: Harbour, 1992.

Tomeatto, Kelly. *Shishalh Stories : A Literacy Reader*. Victoria: BC Ministry of Education, Skills and Training, 1997.

Turner, Nancy J. *Food Plants of Coastal First Peoples*. Victoria/Vancouver: Royal British Columbia Museum/UBC Press, 1995.

Watmough, Don. *Cruising Guide to British Columbia*. Vancouver: Whitecap, 1975-1991.

White, Howard. *Raincoast Chronicles First Five*. Madeira Park: Harbour, 1975.

White, Howard. *Raincoast Chronicles Six-Ten*. Madeira Park: Harbour, 1983.

White, Howard. *Writing in the Rain*. Madeira Park: Harbour, 1990.

White, Howard. *The Sunshine Coast: from Gibsons to Powell River.* Madeira Park: Harbour, 1996.

Wolferstan, Bill. "Sunshine Coast: Fraser Estuary and Vancouver to Jervis Inlet." In *Pacific Yachting's Cruising Guide to British Columbia: Vol III.* Toronto: Maclean-Hunter, 1982.

Wolferstan, Bill. "Sunshine Coast, Fraser Estuary and Vancouver to Jervis Inlet." In *Cruising Guide to British Columbia: Vol III,* Vancouver: Whitecap, 1992.

Wolferstan, Bill. "Sunshine Coast, Fraser Estuary and Vancouver to Jervis Inlet." In *Cruising Guide to British Columbia: Vol III,* Revised Edition. Vancouver: Whitecap, 1995.

Wyngaert, Francis J. Van Den. *The West Howe Sound Story.* Vancouver: Pegasus, 1980.

Appendix 2

Dining on the Sunshine Coast

B:	Burgers	CB:	Coffee Bar	C:	Chicken
CH:	Chinese	ED:	Eclectic/Deli	E:	European
FC:	Fish & Chips	FD:	Formal Dining	F:	French
G:	Greek	I:	Italian	J:	Japanese
M:	Mexican	MD:	Mediterranean	P:	Pizza
SB:	Subs	S:	Seafood	SS:	Soup & Sandwich
T:	Thai	V:	Vegetarian	W:	Western

RR: Reservations recommended.

A & W Restaurant
   665 Mahan, Gibsons   604-886-9669   *B/C*
Angelo's Pizza & Donairs
   5653 Wharf, Sechelt   604-740-9899   *I/C/P/SB*
Apolonia Palace Restaurant
   5584 SC Hwy, Sechelt   604-740-0660   *G/S/P*
Backeddy Marine Pub
   16660 Backeddy, Egmont   604-883-3614   *B/C/FC/W*
Beach Buoy Waterfront Restaurant (Seasonal)
   Davis Bay   604-884-3715   *FC/B*
Big Mac's Deli
   5583 SC Hwy, Sechelt   604-885-0466   *C/P/ED*
Blackfish Pub
   895 Gibsons Way, Gibsons   604-886-6682   *FC/B/C/W*
Blue Heron Inn
   5591 Delta, Sechelt   604-885-3847   *FD/F/S   RR*
Chez Philippe Restaurant
   1532 Ocean Beach Esplanade, Gibsons   604-886-2188   *FD/F/S*
Col Flounders Drive-in
   4326 Garden Bay Road (June to Sept)   604-883-2451   *FC/B*

Creekhouse Restaurant
1041 Roberts Creek Rd, Roberts Creek   604-885-9321 *FD/I Fri, Sat & Sun only*
Daily Roast
5547 Wharf, Sechelt   604-885-4345   *CB*
De Dutch Pannekoek House
895 Gibsons Way, Gibsons   604-886-9090   *Breakfast/B/C*
Drinks 'N Links
Trail Bay Mall, Sechelt   604-885-7846   *ED*
Flying Cow Catering Co & Bistro
451 Marine Dr, Gibsons   604-886-0301   *ED/V*
Flying Saucer, Trail Bay Mall
Sechelt   604-885-3009   *CB*
Flying Saucer Sunnycrest Mall
Gibsons   604-886-3003   *CB/SS*
Garden Bay Hotel Pub
Garden Bay   604-883-2674   *S/FC/B/C*
Garden Bay Hotel Restaurant
Garden Bay   604-883-9919   *S/C/W Open at 5 pm*
Gilligan's Pub Co. Ltd.
5770 SC Hwy, Sechelt   604-885-4148   *B/C/FC*
Golden City Restaurant
5550 Wharf, Sechelt   604-885-2511   *CH/W*
Gumboot Garden Cafe
1057 Roberts Creek Rd, Roberts Creek   604-885-4216   *ED/SS*
Haus Uropa Restaurant
426 Gower Point, Gibsons   604-886-8326   *FD/E*
Hong Kong Sunny Café
Sunnycrest Mall, Gibsons   604-886-3421   *CH/B*
Howl At The Moon
450 Marine Dr, Gibsons   604-886-8881   *M/S/W*
Irvines Landing Marine Pub
Irvines Landing   604-883-2296 (Seasonal)   *S/FC/B/C*
Jack's Lane Bistro & Bakery
546 Gibsons Way, Gibsons   604-886-4898   *G/V/ED*
Jolly Roger Inn
Secret Cove   604-885-7860   *B/FC/C/S/W*
Kafe Amigo
4-5685 Cowrie, Sechelt   604-740-0080   *M/V/CB*
Keeper's Place
5764 Wharf, Sechelt   604-885-4994   *S/B/C/W*
Leo's Mediterranean Tapas & Grill
274 Gower Pt, Gibsons   604-886-9414   *S/MD/W*
Lighthouse Pub
5764 Wharf, Sechelt   604-885-9494   *S/FC/B/C/W*

Lord Jim's Resort Hotel
    5356 Ole's Cove, Halfmoon Bay   604-885-7038   *S/I/W*
McDonald's Restaurant
    5615 SC Hwy, Sechelt   604-885-1005   *B/C*
McDonald's Restaurant
    1100 SC Hwy, Gibsons   604-886-1624   *B/C*
Molly's Reach Restaurant
    647 School Rd, Gibsons   604-886-9710   *S/FC/B/C/P/W*
Mosaic Marketplace Tearoom
    Davis Bay   604-740-0047   *Quiche, Chicken Pie & V*
OThai Restaurant
    5760 Teredo, Sechelt   604-740-5999   *T*
Old Boot Eatery
    5530 Wharf, Sechelt   604-885-2727   *I/P*
Old Country Fish & Chips
    446 Marine Dr, Gibsons   604-886-9707   *FC*
Opa Japanese Restaurant
    281 Gower Pt Rd, Gibsons   604-886-4023   *Sushi Bar J/S*
Pack Ratt Louie's Grill
    818 Gibsons Way, Gibsons   604-886-1646   *S/FC/B/C/P/W*
Panago Pizza
    682 SC Hwy, Gibsons   604-310-0001   *P*
Patra 2 for 1 Pizza
    706 Gibsons Way, Gibsons   604-886-7671   *I/C/P*
Pearl's Homestyle Bakery
    5639 Cowrie, Sechelt   604-885-3395   *ED/P*
Pebbles Restaurant
    Trail Ave, Sechelt   604-885-5811   *S/FC/W*
Pepper Creek Pizza
    Wilson Creek   604-885-0321   *I/C/P*
Pesca Fresca
    Teredo Square, Sechelt   604-885-2363   *ED/S*
Pier 17
    Davis Bay   604-885-9721   *ED/CB*
Pizza Pantry
    12380 SC Hwy, Pender Harbour   604-883-2543   *P/SB/C/Meat Pies*
Poseidon Restaurant
    Wilson Creek   604-885-6046   *G/S/W*
Prontos Grill House
    5547 Wharf, Sechelt   604-885-1919   *G/S/B/C/P/W*
Ruby Lake Resort Ltd.
    Sunshine Coast Hwy, Pender Harbour   604-883-2269   *FD/I/S*
Santosha's Restaurant
    IGA, Gibsons Pk Plaza, Gibsons   604-886-3572   *ED/MD*

Sea Breeze Café	
Trail Bay Mall, Sechelt 604- 740-5686	*SS*
Seaview Gardens	
418 Marine Dr, Gibsons 604-886-9219	*CH/W*
Sechelt 2 for 1 Pizza	
5580 Wharf, Sechelt 604-740-9901	*I/P*
Seiner's Café	
12671 SC Hwy, Madeira Park 604-883-0023	*S/FC/B/C/W*
Strait Coffee Traders	
Wilson Creek 604-885-9757	*SS/CB*
Subway	
Trail Bay Centre, Sechelt 604-885-1026	*SB*
Subway	
Sunnycrest Mall, Gibsons 604-886-0440	*SB*
Sun Fish Café	
5530 Wharf, Sechelt 604-885-0237	*S/V/W*
Sundowner Inn	
4339 Garden Bay Road, Garden Bay 604-883-9676	*I/S/W*
Sunny Crust Bakery	
900 Gibsons Way, Gibsons 604-886-7441	*Pastries*
Tim Hortons	
1078 Gibsons Way, Gibsons 604-886-0882	*CB/Doughnuts/SS*
Tom & Sherry's Place	
16540 SC Hwy, Egmont 604-883-9412	*FC/B/C/W*
Trudy's Place	
923 Gibsons Way, Gibsons 604-886-0864	*ED/CB/P*
Village Restaurant	
Cowrie St, Sechelt 604-885-4515	*S/W*
Wakefield Inn	
6529 SC Hwy, Sechelt 604-885-7666	*B/S/W*
Waterfront Restaurant	
440 Marine Dr, Gibsons 604-886-2831	*B/FC/W*
Wendy's Restaurant	
1078 Gibsons Way, Gibsons 604-886-0822	*B/C*
Robbies Pancakes	
851 Gibson Way, Gibsons 604-886-9090	*Breakfast/B/W*
Wharf Ichiban Restaurant	
4748 SC Hwy, Davis Bay 604-885-7285	*Sushi J/S/W*
Wild Flour Bakery	
5530 Wharf, Sechelt 604-740-9998	*Pastries/P*

Appendix 3

Sunshine Coast Marinas

B:	Bait	BL:	Boat Launch	BR:	Boat Rentals
C:	Charts	CH:	Charters	FD:	Fuel Dock
FL:	Fishing Licenses	G:	Groceries	HO:	Haul Out
I:	Ice	L:	Laundromat	LS:	Liquor Store
M:	Moorage	M:	Mechanic	MS:	Marine Supplies
P:	Propane	R:	Restaurant	SH:	Shower
T:	Tackle	W:	Ways	WR:	Washrooms

Bathgate's Store & Marina, Egmont   604-883-2222
BR/C/CH/FD/FL/G/I/L/LS/P/M/MC/MS/T/SH/W/WR
Buccaneer Marina & Resort, Secret Cove   604-885-7888
B/BL/BR/C/FD/FL/W/HO/I/M/MC/MS/P/T/W/WR
Choquer & Sons, Sechelt Inlet Road   604-885-9244
BL/HO/M/MC/MS/W
Coho Marina, Shark Lane, Madeira Park   604-883-2248
BL/C/CH/FL/I/M/MS/S/T/WR
Egmont Marina Resort, 16660 Backeddy, Egmont   604-883-2298
B/BR/BL/FD/FL/G/I/L/M/MC/R/SH/T/WR
Fisherman's Resort, Garden Bay   604-883-2336
B/BL/BR/C/CH/FL/I/L/M/MC/SH/T/WR
Garden Bay Pub & Marina, Garden Bay   604-883-9919
M/I/R/WR
Gibsons Marina, 675 Prowse, Gibsons   604-886-8686
B/BL/C/CH/FL/HO/I/LM/MS/SH/T/WR/
Headwater Marina, Wilkinson, Pender Harbour   604-883-2406
B/BL/FD/FL/I/M/SH/T/WR
Hyak Marina, 377 Gower Pt, Gibsons   604-886-9011
B/FD/FL/HO/I/MS/T/W/WR/

Irvines Landing Marina, Irvines Landing   604-883-2296
   B/BL/CH/FD/FL/HO/I/M/MS/PUB/SH/T/WR
John Henry's Marina, Garden Bay   604-883-2253
   Annual Moorage/B/C/CH/FD/FL/G/I/LS/P/MS/R/T
Leslie's Marina, 5997 Inlet Ave, Sechelt   604-885-2056
   Annual Moorage only
Mackenzie's Marina, 5878 Marine Way, Sechelt   604-885-7851
   Moorage
Madeira Marina, Madeira Park Road   604-883-2266
   C/HO/I/L/MC/MS/T/W/WR
Poise Cove Marina, 5991 Sechelt Inlet Rd, Sechelt   604-885-2895
   Moorage/BL
Port Stalashen, Wilson Creek   604-885-7792
   Moorage
Royal Reach Motel & Marina, Wharf Rd, Sechelt   604-885-7844
   Moorage
Secret Cove Marina Ltd., 5411 Secret Cove, Halfmoon Bay   604-885-3533
   B/C/CH/FD/G/I/LS/M/MS/SH/T/WR
Silver Sands Resort Ltd., 12077 Bryan, Madeira Park   604-883-2630
   B/BL/BR/C/CH/G/HO/I/L/M/MS/SH/T/W/WR
Sportsman Marina & Resort, #2-13172 Sexw Amin, Garden Bay
   604-883-2479   *Moorage*
Tillicum Bay Marina, 5794 Naylor, Sechelt   604-885-2100
   BL/M/WR

Appendix 4

Sunshine Coast Parks

FP:	Forestry Park	GP:	Gibsons Municipal Park
PP:	Provincial Park	RD:	Regional District Park
SN:	Sechelt Nation Park	SP:	Sechelt Municipal Park

BL:	Boat Launch	CT:	Caretaker on Site
DA:	Disabled Access	DR:	Drinking Water
FL:	Flood Lights	H:	Hiking
MA:	Marine Access Only	PG:	Playground
PT:	Picnic Tables	RR:	Reservations Required
RVC:	RV Camping	SF:	Sports Field
SH:	Showers	SS:	Sani Station
SW:	Swimming	T:	Toilets
TC:	Tent Camping	VA:	Vehicle Access

Armours Beach, Marine Crescent, Gibsons
    GP: PT/SW/VA
Beach Esplanade, Roberts Creek Rd, Roberts Creek
    RD: DW/PT/SW/T/VA
Brothers Memorial Park, Park Rd,Gibsons
    GP: DW/PG/PT/SF/VA
Buccaneer Bay Marine Park, Thormanby Island
    PP: H/MA/SW/T/TC
Chaster House, Ocean Beach Esplanade, Gibsons
    RD: DW/PT/T/VA
Cliff Gilker Park, Roberts Creek
    RD: CT/DA/DW/FL/H/PG/PT/SF/T/VA
Connor Park, Northwood Rd, Halfmoon Bay
    RD: DW/H/PT/PG/SF/T/VA

Coopers Green, Fisherman Rd, Halfmoon Bay
RD: BL/CT/DA/DW/PG/PT/SW/T/VA
Dan Bosch Park, Hwy 101, Ruby Lake
RD: CT/H/PT/SW/T/VA
Davis Bay Waterfront, Davis Bay
SP: SH/SW/T/VA
Dougall Park, Dougall Ave, Gibsons
GP: PG/PT/T/VA
Frances Point Marine Park, Pender Harbour
PP: Under Construction
Garden Bay Marine Park, Garden Bay Rd.
PP: DW/PG/PT/SW/T/VA
Georgia Beach Park, Georgia Dr, Gibsons
GP: PT/T/VA
Hackett Park, Trail Ave, Sechelt
SP: DW/PG/PT/SF/T/VA
Harmony Islands, Jervis Inlet
PP: MA
Homesite Creek Caves, SC Hwy, Halfmoon Bay
FP: H
John Daly Park, Garden Bay Road, Pender Harbour
RD: H/PT/VA
Katherine Lake Park, Garden Bay Rd
RD: CT/DA/DW/H/PT/RVC/SH/SW/T/TC/VA
Kinnikinnick Park, Ripple Way, Sechelt
SP: H/PG/SF/T/VA
Marina Park (Seawall), Gower Point Rd, Gibsons
GP: H/PT/VA
Mason Road Park
SP: VA
Oak Street Park, Ocean Beach Esplanade, Gibsons
RD: H/PT/SW/VA
Pender Harbour Ranger Station, Madeira Park
RD: BL/PT/T/VA
Pender Hill, Lee Bay Rd, Irvines Landing
RD: H/VA
Plumper Cove Park, Keats Island
PP: MA/DW/H/PT/SW/T/TC
Porpoise Bay Park, Sechelt Inlet Rd
PP: DA/DW/H/PG/PT/RR/RVC/SS/SH/SW/T/TC/VA
Princess Louisa Marine Park
PP: DW/H/MA/PT/SW/T

Redrooffs Trails & Pier, Redrooffs Rd, Halfmoon Bay
    RD: H/PT/VA
Roberts Creek Park, Hwy 101
    PP: DA/DW/H/PT/RVC/SS/SW/TC/VA
Sargeants Bay Park, Redrooffs Rd
    PP: DA/DW/H/SW/T/VA Wildlife Sanctuary
Sechelt Inlet Marine Parks, Sechelt Inlet
    PP: MA/SW/T/TC
Sechelt Marsh, Wharf Ave, Sechelt
    SP: H/VA Bird Sanctuary
Secret Beach, Gower Pt. Rd, Gibsons
    RD: PT/SW/VA
Skookumchuck Park, Egmont Rd, Egmont
    PP: H/T/VA
Smugglers Cove Marine Park, Brooks Rd, Halfmoon Bay
    PP: H/SW/T/TC/VA
Smith Cove Park, Smith Rd, Langdale
    RD: PT/VA
Snickett Park, Waterfront Boulevard, Sechelt
    SP: PT/SW/VA
Soames Hill Park, Chamberlain Rd, Gibsons
    RD: H/PT/VA
Ted Dixon Memorial Park, Kwetlin Rd, Sechelt
    SN: DW/FL/SF/T/VA
Trout Lake Park, Hwy 101, Halfmoon Bay
    RD: H/SW/T/VA
Whispering Firs Park, Hwy 101, Gibsons
    RD: DA/H/PG/PT/T/VA
White Tower Park, Shaw Rd, Gibsons
    GP: H/VA
Winegarden Park, Gower Pt. Rd, Gibsons
    GP: DW/T/VA

Endnotes

1. The Shashishalhem word for Roberts Creek was Hwah-sam, which translated means "place of large salmon."
2. *Coast News*, April 19, 1956: page 2.
3. British Columbia Institute of Technology.
4. Meaning "our world."
5. Interview with Rosella Leslie, 1990.
6. *Peninsula Times*, March 27, 1974.
7. James Warnock, Oral History Project, Elphinstone Pioneer Museum.
8. Caryl Cameron, Oral History Project, Elphinstone Pioneer Museum.
9. Isabel Gooldrup, Oral History Project, Elphintoen Pioneer Museum.

Index

Photo Credits

Arnold, Reid: 42
Boothroyd Family: 75;
Bruce, Michelle: 60; 61; 62
Cronin, Ambrose: 35
Davies, Marshall: 118 (m)
Elphinstone Pioneer Museum: 22(b); 34 (photo by Helen McCall); 48 (b);
56 (u); 97; 175
Festival of the Written Arts: 68 (u) (photo by Sgt. Julien Dupuis); 68 (b)
Giroux, Art: 125
Icke & Schenk: 14 (b)
Lehmann, L.D.: (121)
Petraschuk, Robi: 115 (b)
Sechelt Community Archives, Helen Dawe Collection: 14(u) (photo by Philip
T. Timms); 14(b); 19; 29 (photo by Gordon Ballantine); 46; 48 (u); 50;
59; 86 (u)(m)(b); 89;
Sunshine Coast Community Services: 95 (ml & mr)
Wells, Elizabeth: 95(b)
All other photos have been provided by the author.

(b: bottom, m: middle, ml: middle left, mr: middle right, u: upper).

Sunshine Coast Notes

Sunshine Coast Notes

Sunshine Coast Notes

Sunshine Coast Notes

Sunshine Coast Notes

Other Sunshine Coast titles

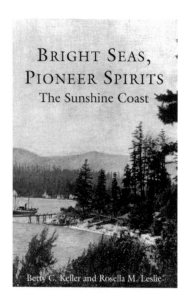

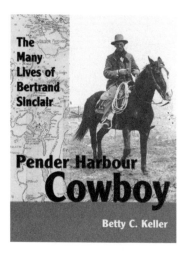

Bright Seas, Pioneers Spirits
The Sunshine Coast
Betty C. Keller and Rosella Leslie

The beautiful Sunshine Coast—that edge of the continent stretching north and west of Vancouver—has been attracting visitors for over a hundred years.

The pioneers were people of courage and daring. Long before coastal roads were built they had turned the winding fiords into highways, reaching out to each other and the world in their boats. Their pioneering spirits still ride the bright seas of the Sunshine Coast.

ISBN 0-920663-44-3 $14.95

Pender Harbour Cowboy
The Many Lives of Bertrand Sinclair
Betty C. Keller

Cowboy, logger, fisherman, writer, social activist and grand adventurer, Bertrand Sinclair's fascinating life is set against a revolution in rural industry.

His story travels from the old west of Montana, California, up to the B.C.'s Sunshine Coast, where he spent 60 years with his beloved boat *Hoo Hoo*. He wrote dozens of novels and hundreds of short stories, four of which became movies.

ISBN 0-920663-72-9 $18.95

Other titles in our "Place to Be" series

Haida Gwaii
The Queen Charlotte Islands
Dennis Horwood and Tom Parkin

When first published in 1989, the authors' *Islands of Discovery* gained instant acclaim as the definitive outdoor guide to the Queen Charlotte Islands.

Now they offer expanded research on the people, culture, and tourist attractions of these magnificent islands.

Known as Haida Gwaii, homeland of the Haida Nation, this magical place is on the must-see list of many travellers.

ISBN 1-895811-78-3 $18.95

Salt Spring Island
A Place to Be
Ellie Thorburn and Pearl Gray

Salt Spring Island has evolved from an occasional native hunting ground to a year round haven for residents and tourists alike. It is now recognized as one of North America's top 100 art colonies.

In this informative keepsake for visitors and residents alike, we meet artists like Robert Bateman and Carol Evans, plus artisans, cooks, pioneers, innkeepers, and naturalists. We learn local secrets and discover quaint B&B accommodations.

ISBN 1-895811-27-9 $16.95

The Author

Rosella Leslie was born in Edmonton, Alberta, graduated from Elphinstone Secondary in Gibsons, and trained as a Medical Records Technician in Merritt, B.C. For eleven years she lived at Clowhom Falls, which is 25 miles by boat from Sechelt, and helped her husband look after a fishing resort. After moving to Sechelt she worked with the Festival of the Written Arts as a director, program writer, and house co-ordinator.

Aided in her writing by weekly critiquint sessions with the Quint-essential Writers Group led by editor and author Betty Keller, Rosella also attended workshops with Ian Slater and Daniel Wood. A winner in the 1986 B.C. Writer's Federation, Best of B.C. Writing Competition, her feature articles and fictional stories have been published in *Western People Magazine Fiction*, *The Leader*, *Alive Magazine* and *Coast News Weekender*. She is co-author with Betty Keller of *Sea-Silver Inside British Columbia's Salmon-Farming Industry* (Horsdal & Schubart, 1996) and a history of the Sunshine Coast: *Bright Seas, Pioneer Spirits*, (Horsdal & Schubart, 1996) for which they won third prize in 1997 B.C. Historical Writing Competition.

Today Rosella lives in Sechelt where she operates the Shady Acres Bed & Breakfast with her husband and son.